"Point your kids in the right direction —
when they're old they won't be lost."

Proverbs 22:6, The Bible, The Message Version

"Friends love through all kinds of weather,
and families stick together in all kinds of trouble."

Proverbs 17:17, The Bible, The Message Version

Dad's Ten Top Lectures, © 2018, Ted Henderson.
Quella Publishing / Amazon Kindle Direct
Englewood, Colorado, USA

The Message Version: The Bible in Contemporary Language
© 2002 by Eugene H. Peterson.

A NOTE ABOUT THIS BOOK

Ted and Julie Henderson are long-time friends of mine. With my wife, Cathy, and six other couples, we have invested in each other's families and spiritual journeys for over twenty years. We have eaten together, traveled together, prayed together, studied together, and guided our children together. Honestly, as a group we have done something very rare and special in our individualistic and private western world: we have chosen to live life in a wonderfully connected yet sometimes crazy way. We learned it from the Bible and call it "koinonia"—from the biblical Greek word meaning "relationship in common." We have been genuinely invited into each other's lives.

As an extremely successful business man, Ted is always full of ideas, questions, and possibilities. He is a man of deep passion, clear convictions, and exceptional drive. Whether it is about faith, piano, sports, government, or finance, Ted has something to contribute. His insightful perspective has fueled our discussions. I have seen Ted soften and grow over the years. There is a gentleness inside him which percolates out. His goodness of character, the size of his heart, and his ability to see the real meaning of life has shaped many of us.

Anyone that Ted knows will comment about his sense of humor. At times it can be unrestrained and politically incorrect, but it is always delivered with a loving twinkle in his eye. When we gather, at some point Ted's dry comments will come, breaking over us like waves on a beach. We laugh until our sides hurt. In December, I wait by the mail box in hopes that Ted's Christmas letter will be dropped off.

Each chapter in this book begins with one of Ted's Christmas letters. The pages in between are unscrubbed Ted. To be invited inside someone's life, with its successes and failures, is a remarkable and miraculous experience. In this book, Ted has been vulnerable and welcomed us all into his family and parenting life, to have "relationship in common." My wish is that by reading *Dad's Top Ten Lectures,* you would join all of us in our Koinonia, too.

FOR THE ROLLING ROCK KOINONIA, 2018
Dr. Brad Strait, Pastor, Cherry Creek Presbyterian Church

Koinonia Christmas at the Hendersons, 2017. From left: Brad, Ken, Ted, Peggy, Julie, Sheri, Jim, Janet, Ross, Lauren, Brett, Joni, and Rusty (Cathy not pictured).

Some of the best looking of our Rolling Rock Koinonia playing in the mud of Dead Sea, Israel, in 2017. Ted is on the right, with Ross, Rusty, Joni, Jim, and Cathy.

Ted's family in 2018: from left: Brett, Jillian, William, Matthew, Audrey, Kelsey (her husband, Brody not pictured), Leah, Ted, and Julie.
Below: Ted in 2017.

INTRODUCTION
DECEMBER 2007

My wife Julie is happy again because I got a real job in October. Life around our house had not been normal since I quit my job in the middle of 2006 with a singular plan in mind - as I turned 50 and faced an empty nest, I wanted to take a year off to write a book about my quarter century journey as a Dad.

Two things made this a bad idea in my wife's eyes. First, I have been the sole financial support for our family for the last twenty-five years. Second, I have never written a book before. The color she turned when I informed her of this plan made Nicole Kidman look like a Hawaiian Tropic model. Obviously, I had some work to do to convince her.

In arguing my case I stated the facts first. "Honey, I am about to turn 50 years old and I hate my job, except for the fact that it comfortably pays the bills. I am completely burned out and I feel like I have earned the right, after 25 years of parenting and providing, to take some time off and try to do something I am passionate about. I know it makes no sense to shut off the income and take a shot at writing a book, but I don't care. The kids are gone which makes it the perfect time for me to try to do this. Worst case I promise I'll have a real job by the end of 2007." (Note that I did secure the job within the promised timeframe, thus saving the marriage.)

Julie looked catatonic, so I continued, "In the meantime, I want to try to create something that I can pass down to the children so they will have some idea about what was going through my mind when I showed up as their Dad. Then they can pass it down. Our grandkids and great grandkids will know who we were and what we were thinking about as parents. Don't you think that would be cool?"

I paused, looking for some support and received nothing from my wife. Panic time. I had to play my ace in the hole, the Oprah Card. You see, for many women like my wife, Oprah is the Oracle and I have invoked her many times in arguments when I thought it would help my cause. This time it was a complete no brainer since there was no question that Oprah would endorse this decision. I knew that at some point I would have to summon the Oracle to sell idea to Julie, I just hadn't expected it to be so soon.

Into the teeth of her stricken silence, I dealt my ace, "Well I know that Oprah would support this decision. There is absolutely no question she would enthusiastically say 'Go for it, Ted!' and probably give me a car. You know she would. Oprah would definitely agree that at this point in my life I should quit the job I hate, take a year off, and write the book I am passionate about." I stopped because that was all I had, my best shot. WWOD? Powerful. I waited.

I watched as my wife actually became Oprah for a minute. She ignored all reason and rationale and went purely on emotion as I hoped she would. She hugged me, took my hands in hers, looked into my eyes and said, "Okay. I know you have been unhappy in your job for a while and you have hung in there. So, I agree with you. I think you should write your book."

This was the first time in about 20 years that I had heard my wife say, "I agree with you," so I was a bit stunned. I quickly recovered and realized that she had just decided to let me do something that went against every fiber in her being. Her supportive response reminded me that I truly love her despite the fact that she has been playing devil's advocate to virtually everything I think, say, or do for quite a long time.

So, I quit my job in the middle of 2006 and wrote the book that follows, much to the chagrin of my own Dad, whose antipathy toward the book made Julie look positively bullish. I had expected Julie to be the one most mortified by the "quit my job, write a book, and figure out the rest later" plan. Nope. It was my 82-year-old Dad, a world class worrier, who really despised this notion. Frankly, he thought I had completely lost it. So, to further aggravate him, I am dedicating this book to my father.

As the title implies, this book is about my Dad and his life lectures and how I passed them on to the next generation. My own childhood experience was that while my Mom ran the comfortable nest of home every day, on weekends and in the evenings my Dad showed up with an agenda to prepare my brother, sister, and I for life outside of that comfortable nest. As I matured, I learned that my Dad viewed his responsibilities very simply: be there unconditionally for the family, support them financially, and hammer home life's basic rules to the kids.

His goal was to get us ready to leave the home and pursue happiness in our lives independently. He believed that if we were equipped with the basics, his definition of a life survival kit, we would eventually leave, succeed on our own, and come back with the grandkids for him and Mom to play with. Dad's weapon of choice in communicating the basics was the lecture.

Initially, it seemed like all of his speeches were different, primarily because the reason we were being preached to was always different. However, as time wore on, it became clear that the sermons were anything but different. On the contrary, they were always the same items being drilled home, with a different wrapping depending on what we had done to warrant the lecture. There really were only about ten points in all, and they were adjusted to fit almost any situation. With this simple view Dad intended to illuminate a path along which his children could achieve contentment in their lives, independently of their parents. In complete panic, I plagiarized whatever I could from him when I became a clueless Dad myself at the age of 25.

I want readers to understand that this book is not intended to be a 'parenting book' in the classic sense of making everyone who reads it feel lousy about what they have done as parents. I have been a parent for well over 20 years and I would never pre-suppose to advise current or prospective parents on how to raise their children. I understand from experience that there is no sure-fire formula for success in the job and no guarantees that specific efforts will yield desired results. There are simply way too many variables that are completely beyond the parent's control that can impact (positively and negatively) a child's life as they grow up. A lot of luck comes into play and parents often get too much credit when their kids succeed and too much blame when they fall short. The kids themselves have a lot to do with how their lives turn out and the parents are along for the ride in many ways.

However, there is no question that a parent, flawed as they probably are, can slant the playing field in the child's favor by showing up and trying to do a good job for their children. To fight the good fight. That is what this book is all about. Beyond a love letter to my parents, my wife, and my children, I wanted to write this book as a tribute to the simplicity of making the effort, like I know millions of Dads are doing every day. Every good Dad that I have ever met has two things in common: (1) they are wholly unprepared for the task at hand and (2) they show up anyway. My own journey started a quarter century ago.

HAPPY HOLIDAYS FROM THE HENDERSONS

Well, after a few years together with Julie, this year I've decided to sit down and write a letter as my contribution to the annual Henderson Christmas card effort. I figured that writing a single letter was going to be easier than dealing with Julie's insistence that I jot personal notes on over 100 cards, which I have done for the previous three years, and hated. I can never come up with anything beyond, "We hope your holidays are really happy!!"

The main problem with a letter like this is that I can't put down typical Ted thoughts like "Did you hear the one about the two nuns and the Doberman?" I've got to take a reasonable holiday tone or my editor (Julie) will nix this and I'll again be resigned to manually saying "We hope your holidays are really happy!!" So, with that in mind here goes.

It is appropriate that this is the first Henderson Christmas Letter as 1982 is the first year we have any interesting news to share with you since Julie and I got married in late 1979. The news? We now have a baby. Brett Edward was born on July 14th, 1982 after we barely made it to the hospital because Julie didn't recognize she was in labor for about 10 hours. Brett is healthy and happy and annoyed by Cinnamon, our 2-year-old golden retriever. The jury is out on how long wildly rambunctious Cinnamon is going to last with children around. She has already almost taken Julie and Brett down a flight of stairs and has knocked me down more than once bolting through the front door in a daily run to daylight. Unfortunately, we messed the dog up pretty good in our trial run as parents – we hope to do better with Brett.

Although Brett isn't capable of much and doesn't really do anything yet but smile, cry, sleep, eat, and mess his diaper, he has somehow managed to reach in and grab my heart in a way that I never imagined possible. I didn't see this coming, but man, do I love being a Dad. My own Dad's reaction to me becoming a father was, predictably, to be concerned. "For crying out loud Ted, we didn't trust you with the dog or the gerbils until a few years ago. Now you are a Dad? I'm sorry, but Mom and I are a bit worried for Brett and our future grandchildren. All we can say is thank God for Julie."

Hey Dad. My response, in language you can understand is, "I'm a Dad now, and I'm showing up."

Julie, of course, saw all of this coming and is thrilled that she is now officially doing what she always dreamed of doing. I can already see what an incredible Mom she is, and I know how lucky I am to have a wife who wants to be at home with the children everyday. She quit her job when Brett was born and the look in her eyes says she is never going back. We have of course discussed this, and the current plan is for her to stay at home and be with the kids while I provide the income. (Yeah Dad, you read that right. Mom, pick Dad up off the floor please. His middle son is officially a grown up and is taking some responsibility.)

Ending this first Christmas letter is easy and predictable. "We hope your holidays are really happy and that you have a healthy 1983!"

Love, Ted, Julie and Brett

CHAPTER 1
I'M SHOWING UP

Like all Dads, my life changed forever the day my first child was born. I have been a complete mess ever since. I am a worrier, which is probably the worst thing a parent hoping to escape insanity can claim. Ultimately, I blame my own Dad for this, as there is no question that I inherited the "worry gene" directly from him. Dad was a child of the Great Depression and saw his family's entire life turned upside down in the early 1930s. The simple lesson that Dad learned as a child was that things in life could change dramatically for the worse in a very short period of time. His personality and approach to life reflected this upbringing; my Dad was a serious man who viewed life as a serious journey where you needed to be prepared for the inevitable bumps in the road.

Throughout his life of responsibility, Dad always seemed to worry that things might change for the worse at any moment, and he guarded against that possibility with a passion when it came to his kids. It was impossible to grow up around Dad and not recognize that he was always a bit worried, a bit on edge, about something, about almost anything. Even if we were doing something as mundane as standing in line at a Dairy Queen, there was always an impending sense of doom in the air when my Dad was around – "Something *could* go horribly wrong in here," is what his body language and demeanor often indicated.

He recognized these flaws in his personality and brought a sense of humor about himself to the role of Dad. My brother, sister, and I all laughed and, as we grew older, teased Dad about how he overreacted to relatively small stuff at times or how he over lectured to make a point. Importantly, Dad was capable of laughing at himself along with us, willing to acknowledge his personal flaws to his children. His self-deprecating sense of humor coupled with the ministrations of my Mother softened what was a serious, disciplined, and potentially intimidating man into a wonderful Dad. Like all good Dads, mine was a flawed human being who would show up and do his consistent best to prepare his children for a life of responsibility and contribution.

It is interesting to note that I didn't even recognize that I had inherited the worry gene from my Dad until I was about to become a parent myself. Until the responsibility of parenting my own children arrived there was literally nothing in my admittedly insulated life that I needed to worry about - things were going along just fine, thank you very much. My parents had nurtured me through my baby, adolescent, and young adult years without life altering incident. After my high school graduation in 1975, I left the comfortable nest of our home in suburban Chicago for southern Alabama, where I had earned a four-year athletic scholarship to play basketball for Auburn University.

The basketball scholarship supports the notion that I have always been somewhat of an over achiever because, as a Division I college basketball player, I absolutely sucked. I had no business playing major college basketball in the Southeastern Conference, surrounded at Auburn by six guys who would eventually play in the NBA, yet I had somehow earned a full scholarship to do just that.

The coaches realized that I was no good early, and I hardly ever played in any games and never scored a point. My career highlight is to be able to say, "I warmed up against Kentucky in front of 23,000 people at Rupp Arena the first year the facility opened." I was one of the two white guys that seem populate the end of the bench on most major college basketball programs in the country. Here is where I sat on the bench: past the five coaches, past the four or five bench guys who actually play in the game, past the manager, past two trainers, past the 8 year old son of the deep pocket alumni, past the injured guys who are wearing suits and can't play, – I mean the very end of the bench. Even if the coach wanted to put me in, it was doubtful he could get my attention.

The result of sucking so bad was that I was forced to sit right next to where the opposing team's cheerleaders performed. I played in the SEC, so this was really not bad duty at all. As I watched the male cheerleaders hoist these breathtakingly beautiful southern girls above their head with one hand positioned strategically under their cheerleader skirt, I often thought while contemplating life from the end of the bench, "Man - I should have been a cheerleader."

Since my college basketball coach actually introduced me to my wife (long story), and since his decision to sign me paid for my entire college education and essentially funded the down payment on our first house, I felt that he deserved at least one story in the book, so here it is. I recall vividly how impressed I was watching my college coach, Bob Davis, still fret about a game that we were leading by 30 with 2 minutes to play. The look on his face made it clear that he was still coaching this game – he actually looked worried. Suddenly, with under a minute to play he screamed down the bench to me, "Henderson, get in there!"

As I made the trek past the assembled masses that rated higher than I did on the bench, I realized that Coach Davis had relaxed for the first time that night. I connected the dots and came up with this: The reason he looked worried was that he still had one last coaching decision to make – he had to decide whether a 30-point lead with less than two minutes to go was a safe enough lead to put me into the game. After hemming and hawing over this (obviously tough) decision for over a minute, he made the decision that even I couldn't blow a 30-point lead all by myself with under a minute to go, so he called my name.

I checked in with 40 seconds to play and immediately fouled someone so I could get into the scorebook. I remember thinking, "Sweet. I actually played in a Division I college basketball game. And I suck. Cool." I would lean on this over achievement in my athletic career six years later, when I realized that I would need to seriously overachieve if I had any hope of becoming a good Dad.

Anyway, I took advantage of the athletic scholarship, made decent grades as an accounting major at Auburn, graduated without owing anybody any money and secured a job with a (then) Big 8 accounting firm in Denver, Colorado - Arthur Andersen & Company. During this time, I also met and fell in love with my wife, Julie. After we graduated, we got married, moved to Denver and bought our first house, courtesy of the money the basketball scholarship had allowed me to save.

I didn't plan any of this. I was just taking the next logical step as it seemed to present itself. This all might have been different if I had not fallen in love at such an early age, but I did, so Julie and I started building our life together in Denver in 1979 at the age of 22. She was pregnant with Brett less than three years later and I was approaching becoming a Dad the same way I had approached everything else in my life, with no worries and a confidence that everything would be just fine - a true sign that I was, in fact, clueless.

Brett himself underscored this fact for me while he was spending time at our house over Christmas in 2005. He was 23 at the time. He was looking at our wedding picture and asked, "So Dad, you are 22 in this picture, right?"

I answered, "Uh-huh. Both Mom and I are 22 in that picture."

He continued, "And you had me when you were 25, right?" I nodded. "And you had Matt and Kelsey by the time you were 30, right?"

"Uh huh."

He smiled and started slowly shaking his head as he placed the picture down, "Man, I am not even close to being ready to get married, let alone have a kid!"

Still being Dad, I took the opportunity to make a critical parenting point, "Whenever you decide to do those things, make sure you do them in that order, okay?"

The truth is I was clueless before I became a Dad; I was clueless as a husband first. When I stood next to my wife at the altar in 1979, I didn't even know that I was marrying a Democrat. Political stuff just didn't come up when I was chasing her around in college and we were falling in love. Had I known that in the 1976 Presidential election, the first in which we were both eligible to vote, she voted for Jimmy Carter, things might have turned out differently, but it just didn't come up. Obviously, it has come up since. My wife and I don't agree on everything, and our children have been exposed to proper political dissent within our home throughout their lives.

In fairness, my wife didn't know what she was getting into with me either. In addition to finding out that she had landed a rather conservative Republican as her husband, she also was surprised to find that, as a companion to my acknowledged passion and energy, I had a bit of a temper problem. This character flaw was somewhat manageable, as my temper generally flared on the athletic field when I was still playing in sports leagues early in our marriage, or when I was coaching the kids later on.

In addition to my temper, I brought impatience to our life together and, since my impatience frequently triggered my temper, this became a bit of a problem for us also. I unsuccessfully tried to argue that these traits served me well in my efforts to provide for the family. Julie made it very clear that there was no excuse for abominable behavior in our home and if I needed those traits to provide, I better make a good transition from work by the time I got home every night. I think that this was the exact moment where she established herself as the "boss of me."

The fact that I was a worrier wasn't really a problem for us early in our marriage. My worrying was borne out of my concerns about parenting and providing and therefore didn't emerge until we had been together for a few years and had a couple of kids. Had Julie known that a dormant worry gene was awaiting the stress of parenting to awaken within me things might have turned out differently for her also. The point is, fresh out of college, there was a lot that Julie didn't know about me and a lot that I didn't know about her, yet we were about to begin a life together as husband and wife.

What we did know about each other was that we were in love (and lust) and on the exact same page when it came to how we looked at faith, family, and raising kids. Not surprisingly, that has been more than enough to sustain us. I have yet to identify any real flaws in her except that she is a Democrat. Her list of my flaws is quite long and, as a true modern-day Democrat, she doesn't offer any constructive solutions, she just constantly points them out.

Looking back to the starting point for all these significant changes in my life, I was completely unaware about the long-term impact that they were going to have on me. This wasn't because I was stupid - I

15

was just young. I had happily stumbled through my youth to the age of 22 at a pretty comfortable pace and I naively figured life would continue that way for me. Over the next 8 years the pace would accelerate dramatically as I would get married, take a 70 hour a week job, buy a house, have three children, change careers, buy a bigger house, etc. Once my worry gene was sparked over concerns about my abilities as a Dad and a provider, it was virtually impossible to turn it off. It kicked in about 25 years ago and has not been in the off position since.

What initially triggered my worry gene a quarter century ago was, interestingly enough, parenting books. I began worrying that I wasn't going to be a good Dad when I started reading parenting books a few months before Brett arrived. Some of these books had quick quizzes that were supposed to indicate what kind of a Dad you would be. My scores always indicated that I should try my luck with a pet first. What I took from these books was that a good Dad should "Be patient and have a level demeanor, he should never lose his temper, he should not be a worrier or a complainer, he should relax and not panic in a crisis." As I had absolutely none of these traits, I quickly came to the conclusion that the resume I was bringing to the table was a pretty lackluster one.

In addition to my poor resume, I was horrible with babies. One of our best friend couples had started having their kids about a year before us, so I got to be around a newborn pretty frequently when we were pregnant with our first child. I was just awful with him. Young David Joslyn always cried whenever I held him, probably because I held him like he was a nuclear device. I just didn't have any experience with babies and I didn't know how to act, so I tried to make him laugh and smile and always failed miserably. Baby David hated me.

What really hurt was how much he loved and accepted my wife. She could take him, hold him, rock him and goo-goo with him and he would be perfectly content. I would take him from her and try to do the exact same things and he would start to scream bloody murder within a few seconds of being in my arms. It was clear. According to the experts, represented by the parenting books and an actual baby, I was going to be a lousy Dad. I began to worry.

16

This fear of failure acted as it often has in my life, it motivated me. I set out to prove the experts wrong. To this day, I can remember the moment, sitting on the couch with my wife, mindlessly paging through parenting books about two months before Brett would be born, when I committed to show up. Damn the experts, I was going to show up and be the best Dad I could be.

One of the (apparently few) good things about my personality is that, when I am motivated and committed, I prepare for the challenge at hand and am disciplined enough to see things through. The fact that this mindset was already a part of my personality was a good thing since, in a marriage with children, there is no option to quit. We had excitedly decided to start our family months earlier and there was no turning back now, so I set out to *prepare* to be a good Dad and see the task through to the end, despite all my personality flaws.

Like all prospective parents, my wife and I sat around in the months before our first child arrived and contemplated names and shared our big picture hopes and dreams with each other. As usual on these broad life strokes, we were simpatico, and we talked about our as yet unborn children endlessly. What we wanted for them was basically what we had experienced ourselves growing up.

Julie and I both had happy childhood, adolescent, and young adult memories that were anchored by an involved Mom at home and an involved Dad who worked to support the family. We both eagerly gave credit to our parents for any and all achievements that we might count at this point in our lives. They had prepared us to live happy, independent, and productive lives and in doing so had left a roadmap for us as prospective parents.

So, we started preparing to be parents by listing the positive, big picture traits that we believed we possessed as a direct result of our own parents. We obviously wanted to remember these things, how they were imparted to us, and make sure to pass them on to our own children. What we came up with were foundation things like, faith, living a balanced life, an understanding of rights and responsibilities, and a passion for life where you showed up every day. These were

17

the basics as I remembered them from my own Dad's lectures when I was growing up and Julie had heard similar logic from her parents. The foundation list was nothing more than a common-sense message that supported the notion of building a strong base under the child that they could lean on for their entire life.

While we were crafting this foundation list, I remembered something else my Dad had often said to me when I was a teenager, long after much of the foundation stuff listed above had already been built. Dad always operated from a worst-case scenario and he would say, "No matter how strong your foundation is, never forget how vulnerable we are as human beings. That is especially true as a teenager, when you still lack life experience but essentially participate as an adult. You are not bulletproof. As a teenager, you are going to be exposed to many things and Mom and I are not going to be there to tell you what to do – or what not to do. We hope that we have passed on the concept of good judgment to you, because all of that comes home to roost during the teenage years. You will encounter things that if not handled properly, could result in the end of your life. The teenage years are serious times and everything you have worked for, all the solid foundation stuff you have built, can be lost in an instant of bad judgment. You have to stay alive during the teenage years to enjoy your life as an independent adult. Am I getting through to you here?" Um, yeah, thanks for that dark bolt of lightening, Dad. Beyond a mental note, I burned out a parental neuron that was the seed of the staying alive lectures.

These pre-child talks with my wife were the origin of Dad's Top Ten Lectures. Through these conversations, and my history with my own Dad, I identified the foundation, staying alive and real-world lecture categories before we even had our first child. I also remember these conversations as the beginning of my confidence build as a Dad. After a discussion like this with my wife, I would say to myself, "If I just show up and make a real effort, I am going to be a decent parent. I can teach the basic foundation stuff that we went through tonight through lectures. I will not be naïve or afraid to talk candidly to my kids about the dangers of the teenage years – I lived them too. I will provide financially for this family. Things are going to be okay as long as I show up."

So, I was committed to show up, which was a start. However, because of my tendency to over achieve when I commit to something, I proceeded to show up and insert myself into every possible parental situation over the next 25 years whether I was invited or not. This annoyed both my wife and my children because, with my black and white mindset, I approached most situations as problems to be solved, confident that I had the solution somewhere in my arsenal of lectures. Unfortunately, often there was no problem until I arrived.

Later in our marriage, my wife said to me, "Honey, I know that you are big on showing up and you are trying to be a good Dad, and you are — you are a good Dad. However, sometimes when you show up you inadvertently make things worse. Not everything is a big problem that needs to be solved. Sometimes you jump in the middle of things without thinking and splash mud on everyone around you. You create a problem, or you make a little problem worse and then you have to clean up." Some sensitivity in her voice showed up and she took my hand and smiled at me, "You sometimes try too hard and you make things a little messy. Try not to be so messy. Okay?"

Since she was being kind of nice to me, I pulled her towards me and said seductively, "I'd like to get messy with you right about now." She pushed me back and rolled her eyes at me then turned to walk away. For some reason, my timing in hitting on my wife was always a bit off after we had kids.

The point is when I committed to show up with my lecture platform, that meant my family was going to get all of me — the good and the bad. As an aside, I acknowledge that the term lecture has a negative connotation for many since it implies a one-sided oratory where there is no give and take. In other words, the child does not get to be heard while the parent pontificates, usually to instruct or admonish specific behavior.

My view of this was, "Are you kidding me? I am Dad and I have a job to do here. I remember being a kid — they are generally oblivious and need a whole lot of guidance and direction. I am not trying to fit into some expert's view of how parent/child interaction should play out. I am going to show up every day, rely on my own specific knowledge of my children, and apply common sense as best I can. I am trying to prepare three children that I love more than anything in the world for their future – and there are no trial runs. I get one shot, over a relatively short period of time and I'm not going to screw this up."

So, the kids always knew that I was serious about showing up and doing my job as Dad. They knew Julie was serious about showing up and doing her job too. Mom's Top Ten Lectures were different from mine. Julie would be the driving force behind imparting the everyday basics to our children - honesty, compassion, respect, kindness, courtesy, manners, discipline, and grooming. She would develop the children's moral code and sense of values every day within the confines of the comfortable nest, while my job was to prepare them for an independent life outside of it. This combined Mom and Dad effort seemed to be the best way to ensure that the comfortable nest would eventually become the empty nest.

HAPPY HOLIDAYS FROM THE HENDERSONS

I always thought 1984 was going to be a cool year to experience ever since I read Orwell's "1984" when I was in high school. I was fascinated by the book and by Winston Smith's job at the Ministry of Truth where he re-wrote history to fit Party propaganda. The cynic in me believes that there is a bit of this "re-writing history" in many Christmas letters that we receive each year, and as an author of an annual letter I must admit that there is temptation to make things sound a bit more exciting than they really are each year.

However, this year we have no desire to re-write history or make stuff up. 1984 was a great year for us as we welcomed our second child Matthew Lawrence on February 29. Yes, he was a leap year baby. We are already concerned about the possible blowout 16th birthday party which will be celebrated in leap year 2000.

Brett is now almost 2 ½ and has welcomed his little brother (now 10 months old) with open arms. After I was blindsided by how passionately I fell for Brett, I have to admit that I was concerned if I could possibly have the capacity to love another child as intensely. Amazingly, this has been no problem whatsoever. I am as taken by baby Matthew as I was with baby Brett – and I am loving walking and (kind of) talking Brett more than ever. Julie and I are enjoying every moment with the boys and we are attempting to build a comfortable nest in which they can flourish.

1984 will also be remembered as the year when I changed careers. After four years at Arthur Andersen I have taken a job with Jones Intercable, one of the top operators in the rapidly growing cable industry. Typically, this career change was not well thought out. I simply loved cable as a consumer because of their emerging coverage of the NCAA basketball tournament and felt that the industry might be a good place to build a career. I am excited and enjoying my new job at Jones.

1984 was also a seminal year in our home from a political perspective. Certainly, I don't want to re-write this history. Don't tell her parents, or Democratic stalwart Granny Grace, but Julie voted for President Reagan in November. We tread cautiously around politics in our house ever since we realized (on the honeymoon) that we come from very different political backgrounds and often look at the world quite differently. We will attempt to do political dissent properly in our comfortable nest so the children are exposed to my views as well as Julie's crazy ideas. (I'm just kidding honey.) THIS IS JULIE INSERTING A COMMENT: TED IS CORRECT. WE DO COME FROM DIFFERENT BACKGROUNDS AND WE DO LOOK AT THE WORLD DIFFERENTLY. I AM WORRIED FOR MY CHILDREN.) You see, this is why I have to write the Christmas letter each year. Julie just isn't very funny.

Note that Cinnamon, our enthusiastically wild golden retriever, is not included in the Christmas picture this year. We found a new home for her on a farm where she can run free and play to her hearts content. She was just a bit too wild to have around young children. I promise that we really found new owners for her that live on a farm - we didn't send her to the big dog farm in the sky.

Well, I have finished a page and hopefully not bored you all. We conclude by wishing all of our friends and family a very Merry Christmas, Happy Holidays, and a wonderful New Year ahead in 1985.

Love, Ted, Julie, Brett and Matthew

CHAPTER 2
THE COMFORTABLE NEST

The "comfortable nest" is a term my parents, and then Julie and I, used to describe the reliable home, the safe place where everybody loves one another unconditionally and is there to support each other. The stay-at-home Mom's main task is to build and maintain the comfortable nest while Dad and the children simply occupy and enjoy it, kind of like the dog does.

We wanted to provide a nurturing nest where the children knew that they were loved, and a disciplined nest where the children understood that there was acceptable behavior and unacceptable behavior. We also wanted to contrast the comfort and security of the reliable home with the uncertainty of the real world, so they could adequately prepare for a competitive, independent adult life.

Accordingly, I lectured often about family and the comfortable nest to all three children, generally as a direct off shoot of the balanced life foundation lecture. The primary message was that family trumps everything. "We always want you to trust the input that comes from home. We love you and your siblings love you and we always want what is best for you. What you will hear outside of the comfortable nest may be driven by a totally different agenda than what is best for you. We will always have your best interests at heart, even when it may not seem so to you. We are asking you to trust that simple fact." The consistency with which we showed up year after year eventually brought us some credibility with the kids, and they thankfully trusted the input that was coming from home by the time they reached the tumultuous teen years.

I knew that consistency was critical. When I thought of my own parents, one word came to mind: constant. My parents were a constant in my life as I navigated the waters of my youth and remain a constant today as I approach my fifties. They were not geniuses at parenting, nor did they ever take a class or read a 'how to' book. They just built a comfortable nest, showed up with unconditional love, and applied common sense and discipline in dealing with their children. While growing up, their presence was at times a major pain and at times indescribably comforting, but the constancy never varied. When it came to parenting, my Mom and Dad took to heart the old line that '90% of it is just showing up' and applied it with a regimented vigor for their children.

One of my first agenda items in showing up as Dad was to sell the concept of the comfortable nest to the children, just as my parents had sold it to me. They had to trust it. In doing this I thought it was necessary to make it clear that the real world they would encounter as teenagers and young adults was no comfortable nest. Contrasting the security and comfort of our home with the high school, college, and workplace environments the children would encounter in their young adult years was a big part of the staying alive and real-world lectures. So, I made the point that the comfortable nest didn't really represent reality. "It is a bubble, where you are protected because you are constantly surrounded by your family, those who love you and care about you. You get a whole lot more "do-overs" in the home. Life outside of the comfortable nest is a bit different – and you need to prepare for an adult life in the real world. But we always want you to take comfort and know that within our home you are unconditionally loved by your parents and your siblings. Got it?"

While the children heard about these wonderful concepts hundreds of times, I want to be clear that our home included cage match level battles amongst them. My kids went at it hammer and tong at times, and over the years it was not unusual to hear oldest son Brett frequently say to middle son Matthew, "Matt, I swear I am going to kill you!" in a tone that implied he really meant it. For two brothers that were only 18 months apart, I viewed their confrontations as completely normal, especially given my upbringing with my own older brother. Although my wife worried about how much the kids fought, she found strange comfort in the fact that nothing my kids ever did to each other measured up to the stories I told her about my own childhood.

My older brother Bart can only be described as truly creative in the ways he dominated me. I was almost four years his junior, looked up to him as all little brothers do, and was always hanging around hoping to play with him and his friends. As I improved athletically, I was sometimes invited to be the extra body needed to fill out a team, but when I was younger this was not the case - I was just a pain in his backside. Since he couldn't just continue to pound me into submission (Dad had finally stepped in to stop the beatings I took at some point) my brother often had to get creative to get rid of me.

The following story is an older brother clinic on how to get your younger brother to not want to play with you anymore. I was about 9, and desperately wanted to play "war" with my brother and his friends one fall day after school. I pushed and annoyed my Mom so much that she finally relented and came outside and told Bart that he had to let me play with him. He was clearly disgusted and said, "Fine, he can play war with us."

The moment the door closed behind my Mom, Bart said, "Ted, you are now a prisoner of war."

Unaware if what that meant I said, "Okay."

My brother said, "First we need to build you a prison." We grew up in Chicago and always had firewood stacked up in the fall. My brother ordered his friends to stack these huge logs on their ends in a tight circle. The logs were unstable standing on their ends and I was instructed to step over the logs into my prison. My brother then placed more logs on top of the already standing logs until the prison reached my head – and was even more unstable. They topped it off by laying a log across the top. If I moved and hit a side, the prison would tumble on me like the house of cards that it was, and it would hurt. It hadn't yet dawned on me that all of my brother's friends were present at the prison site and they weren't playing war anymore, they were playing torture Ted.

My brother, satisfied with my confines, then asked me, "Where are the secret plans for the invasion?"

I responded honestly, "What secret plans?"

My brother, "I will try once more. Where are the secret plans for the invasion?"

"What invasion?"

Angrily, "You know what invasion! I am sorry that you won't tell us. Maybe this will help convince you to give us the information we need."

He then walked over our Labrador retriever's dog run and shoveled up a huge pile of dog shit. He menacingly held the shovel up over the top of the prison and said, "One more time, when is the invasion coming?"

Now I kind of understood what was happening, but I wasn't quick enough to help myself. I screamed, "I don't know anything!!"

Down came the dog shit all over me and as I moved to avoid it, I hit the unstable walls and the prison came down on me. I was scratched and bruised by the heavy logs and had dog shit on my arm and in my hair. My brother ordered his friends to hold me while others rebuilt my prison. Everyone seemed to be having a good time but me.

This whole scene was repeated again. I managed not to bring down my prison walls, but I had dog shit all over me. I gave up no information – I didn't have any. Finally, I realized that if I pushed out hard and ran fast, I might avoid the falling logs and escape. I just wanted my Mommy at this point. So, I did just that and managed to break free and start running.

Someone yelled, "Escaped prisoner!!" and before I could get to the house I was chased down and pummeled by a few of my brother's friends.

It was at this point that my brother saw that I had had enough since I was openly crying. He asked as I limped towards the house, "Are you sure you don't want to keep playing with us?"

"No!" I sobbed, and when I was close enough to the door of the house to feel safe, I yelled, "I hate you! You're a jerk."

I entered the house in tears, admittedly shaken, so I am not sure if the following is an accurate depiction of how my Mom reacted, but I think it is close. I stood in the kitchen bloodied and covered in dog shit and stared at my Mom (looking exactly like Laura Petrie from the

"Dick Van Dyke Show") who was cooking dinner. She noticed my presence and turned and said to me, "Hi honey, did you have fun playing war?"

I incredulously looked at her and said, "Noooo! Look at me. They made me a prisoner of war."

She looked at me and didn't say anything about my appearance and simply asked, "Did you give up any information?"

Frustrated I said, "What information? I don't have any information. I am 9!"

She said, "That's my boy. Now you know. War is hell." And she went back to cooking dinner.

I have thought about my POW experience often since the hysteria about Abu Grahib and Guantanamo emerged. I was thankful that my brother was too old to be a prison guard in a post 9/11 world since he obviously would have sullied the family name.

My childhood life mirrored my own parenting situation, as my brother Bart and I had a younger sister who would go pro in 'Tattletale'. Since I was taught that there is nothing worse that a tattletale, I treated my baby sister Holly horribly for most of her young life. In a typical example, my cousin Marcia and I would invite Holly to play hide and seek with us and then we would not look for her for about an hour. We would just let her sit in the closet somewhere thinking she had a great hiding place while we listened to music. Then we would find her, praise her hiding ability, and tell her to hide again – for another hour. She didn't figure out we never really looked for her until she was about 25 years old, a revelation that re-opened some old scars.

The worst thing my brother and I ever did to our baby sister was when we put her two gerbils (Elizabeth and Sophia) on the pool table and shot the pool balls at them. Seeing them scurry away for the balls was funny and often Elizabeth would reach the edge of a pocket and 'Geronimo' into it seeking safety from a ball only to have it fall on top of her in the leather pocket. (I know, someone should call PETA.)

This activity was, in and of itself, entertaining enough for two young boys killing time in a pre-video game world. However, the event became high family theatre when Elizabeth, who apparently had her brains scrambled a bit in the game of pool, completely chewed off Sophia's head later that night. As fate would have it my sister found the carnage and completely freaked out – hyperventilating, feeling faint, I mean the whole nine yards. If anyone tried to reach in to the cage to get Elizabeth, she would try to bite them. Her blood-soaked face snapping at you was actually a pretty scary sight. Elizabeth had to be sent back to the pet store for rehab, or whatever they do to gerbils who have gone crazy and kill other gerbils and try to bite people all the time. The way my sister freaked out there was no way that my brother and I were going to come clean and admit what we had done.

This became one of those classic family stories where my brother and I kept the secret for well over a decade. For the next 15 years we always got really quiet whenever the subject came up about how weird it was that Elizabeth went cannibal on Sophia completely out of the blue. The truth was finally revealed to my sister and parents on a family vacation when everyone was of legal drinking age and had consumed many cocktails. My Dad thought this was possibly the funniest story he had ever heard – he always hated the gerbils anyway. My sister and Mom thought it was awful. My brother and I were relieved to be rid of the secret.

The fact that today my sister only tells nice stories about how I treated her when she was younger (there are only two such stories) is unbelievable. Our close relationship today is a testament to the bond of unconditional love that develops between siblings who were raised together in a comfortable nest. Certainly, I didn't earn the love and trust that she has in me as an adult, it was just a given in the comfortable nest we were raised in.

In our home, Kelsey was the youngest and our only girl, and she played those cards to her advantage against her brothers as often as possible. Like all females, she understood leverage much earlier than either of the boys did and she worked it. For example, she knew that if she screamed as if one of the boys had hurt her, Dad was likely to drop the hammer first and ask questions later. Her emergence as a part time agent for Mom and Dad about anything questionable that the boys might be doing caused the boys to often want to do her harm.

Her ultimate comeuppance came at the hands of her middle brother. Matthew, Kelsey, and Julie were sitting around on a Saturday afternoon waiting to go to the mall to buy some more clothes. (I always argued that the children seemed to have plenty of clothes and really did not need anymore, and I always lost.) Julie announced that she was going to use the bathroom and then they would go shopping. Almost the moment the door to the bathroom shut behind Julie, the telephone rang, and Matthew answered it.

"Hello?" Listening. "Um, she can't come to the phone right now." Listening. "Well, if you really need to know she is in the bathroom." Matthew is smiling a sly smile and laughing silently with co-conspirator Kelsey, who is listening and smiling along.

Matthew again listened and then said, "Well, I think I'd better have her call you when she gets out. She has already been in there a really long time." Listening. "Yeah, I think she must be taking a dump." Kelsey burst out laughing and slapped Matt's knee. He smiled back at her and finished, "Okay, I will have her call you. You know if she ever finishes in there." He hung up and both children laughed together.

Julie came out of the bathroom and asked what was so funny. Kelsey immediately dropped dime on Matthew, "Matt told someone who called that you were in the bathroom taking a dump!"

Julie looked at Matthew questioningly and he calmly said, "Mom, I absolutely did not do that."

Kelsey, "Yes you did. He's lying, Mom. I was sitting right here."

Matthew said, "I'm not lying. What happened was I told *Chris* that *Kelsey* was in the bathroom taking a dump. By the way Kelsey, you need to call Chris when you get a chance." Chris was the first boy who showed interest in Kelsey – at about age 13. Kelsey started screaming and began hitting Matthew who was laughing hysterically.

Accordingly, my kids weren't always happy with each other within the confines of our comfortable nest and (like most siblings) they fought quite a bit. As I mentioned, this fact worried Julie, who apparently came from one of seven homes in the world where there were hardly ever any disagreements. Over the years I have shared many of my own childhood stories with Julie. She was always relieved, in a weird way, to hear that I treated my sister much worse than our boys ever treated Kelsey; and that nothing Brett ever did to Matthew approached the dog shit prison thing that I endured.

A relieved Julie was a good thing because, in a traditional home, the Mom is the CEO and "If she ain't happy..." certainly applied in our comfortable nest. I have always been a bit defensive on my wife's behalf in a world that seems to have diminished the importance of a Mom being at home every day to raise her children. In 1997, I saw an article in USA Today about Hillary Clinton inviting working Moms to the White House to be honored. As I read the article, I thought, "Isn't this what Mother's Day is for, to honor Moms? Why do working Moms need to be singled out over stay-at-home Moms and have a special day at the White House with Hillary?" My reaction was to write an editorial to USA Today defending my wife and stay at home Moms in general.

ALL MOMS WORK (Editorial Page)

I noted with interest a blurb in USA Today that said Hillary Clinton invited 150 mothers to the White House to salute working moms ("Hillary Salutes Working Moms").

To say the label "working mom" infuriates me is an understatement. The implication, although emphatically denied by women's groups, is that stay-at-home mothers don't work.

Stay-at-home mothers not only work but, in many cases, have sacrificed careers for what they believe to be a greater need – raising their children.

I acknowledge economics takes any choice out of the matter for many mothers, single or married. The reality of our times is difficult.

I am not disparaging mothers who choose to work outside their homes not out of economic necessity but to pursue careers and validate their self-worth either. I'm spouting off because lost in this "you can have it all" world are the stay-at-home moms who hold the most important jobs in the country.

There are a large number of very capable, intelligent, and educated women who had the luxury of a choice when they became mothers. They chose to stay at home and raise the children they brought into this world and to impart their beliefs and values to their own children.

These women are my heroes. I suspect they'll never be saluted at the White House, but I don't think they care. They're too busy working.
--- Ted Henderson, Englewood, Colo.

Yes, I got some hugs and kisses from my wife after this was published, but that was short lived. About a week later, we were lying in bed talking and I was obviously distracted. I was focused on trying to cash in physically on the editorial again and wasn't really listening to what Julie was saying. This was obvious to her, aggravated her, and she proceeded to let me know about it. This caused me to get defensive and say, "So basically you are angry with me for being attracted to you? I don't get it. I would think that is a good thing."

She responded, "You don't see how not listening to me and just tolerating me, waiting until I am done talking so you can hit on me is offensive to me and discounts me? You don't see that?"

"No. I am a guy. Of course I don't get that. I see you lying next to me looking great and I get distracted and am plotting my course. And the course I am plotting is not an 'outer course', if you catch my drift."

Not even a smile from her. "Plot all you want. I am telling you that this bothers me to the point of disinterest."

As I lay there realizing I had ruined any chance of physical affection I decided to make things worse by talking some more and said, "You know, I am really an easy-going guy. I don't know why you and I butt heads so often. Everyone else in my life finds me easy going – you don't. Why are you so difficult?"

She sat up in bed and looked at me in stunned silence for a few seconds and then burst out laughing and didn't stop for a while. When she finally regained her composure, she said to me, "Honey, seriously, you want to lay there and tell me that you would describe yourself as easy going?"

I came back defensively because of course I was easy going. "Absolutely. I try to get along with everybody. I almost always go for the laugh. I go along to get along. Yeah, I'm easy going. You're the one who is hard to get along with."

She laughed again and said, "And I promise that you are the only one who sees yourself that way. Easy going? Are you kidding me? You are Ted. I can't believe you would ever make that claim. Honey? C'mon."

In hindsight, I should have taken the opportunity to back off right about here, but because I am an imbecile when it comes to dealing with my wife, I did not. "Okay. How about this? We are going to poll our closest friends and family members and see what they all have to say about this. We'll see if they think I am easy going or not."

Without hesitation she said, "Yeah, let's do that. And we are going to use the exact term 'easy going' in the poll, right?"

"Of course, because I *am* an easy-going guy."

She put her head back down on the pillow and we laid there quietly for maybe a full minute. Then she broke out laughing again and said, "This is going to be so much fun."

Her confidence was becoming a bit unnerving, so I tried to change the subject. I rolled over towards her and leaned against a stiff, unwelcoming frame. "Yes, it is going to be fun. Speaking of fun, I see you working here. It is obvious that you are finding me irresistibly attractive tonight and I know that you want to make out with me before we go to sleep."

She laughed again, pushed me away and said, "I want to make out with easy going Ted, but I have never met him. Why don't you introduce me sometime?"

Needless to say, I lost this argument in an absolute landslide. In fact, my friends and family members all took the opportunity to add their own two cents about why I am not easy going at all.

My brother Bart responded this way, "Ted, easy going? Sure he is, as long as you agree with everything he says and allow him to talk 95% of the time. Yeah, under those circumstances he is really relaxed and tolerant."

My mother this way, "Well, honey, you are a little intense and it is hard to reconcile that with an easy-going label. So, no, I wouldn't describe you that way. But I still love you." Thanks Mom, for no help whatsoever.

My sister Holly reacted just like my wife initially did. She almost peed her pants laughing.

My Dad didn't help at all when he said, "Of course you are easy going, just like I am."

Our best friends went to great lengths to basically describe me as oddly likable but laughed at any suggestion that I was easy going. Multiple friends brought up old stories about my performance on the athletic fields where I got tossed from games for losing my temper. "Relaxed guys don't really act like that. So, no I would never describe Ted that way." Pause and thinking, "I don't really enjoy talking politics with him too much either." Thinking again and then concluding, "Yeah, he is definitely not a very easy-going guy."

After going through this gauntlet, I had the feeling that the only reason our friends kept me around was because I came with Julie. I could almost hear them saying, "We love Julie, and we guess that insufferable Ted is good for a few laughs every once in a while."

I thought to myself after this poll was taken, "No wonder I am always in trouble with Julie in our comfortable nest. I'm apparently not very easy going."

This was a revelation to me because I know that I am more laid-back than my Dad was. I certainly don't remember him being in trouble with Mom as much as I have been with Julie. I drew the obvious conclusion: Wives from the 50's, 60's, and 70's were just cooler and less judgmental than wives today. I blame the feminists.

In our home it was always tougher for me to recover when I was in trouble than it was for the kids. That is because the kids had to *know* that they could get back in their parent's good graces when they screwed up. This contrasts with the husband who is often left dangling, wondering if he can ever get out of the doghouse and receive some affection again. The kids had to *know* they could recover and get out of the doghouse, and of course this means they recovered hundreds of times.

Brett even recovered from completely desecrating the comfortable nest when he was 8 years old. As my oldest and most stubborn child, I often had to send Brett to his room, with the admonition, "I want you to think about this alone in your room for a few minutes and then I will be up to talk to you some more."

Although Brett would dutifully sulk off to his room, he wasn't done fighting his punishment. The moment he arrived at his room, he would shout downstairs, "Can I get a drink of water?" Or, "Dad, I have to go to the bathroom. Can I?" Anything that would help pass the time and allow him to feel as if he had negotiated down his punishment was something he would pursue, and he pursued it often.

I finally had enough of playing this game with him. The next time he got into trouble and was sent to his room he predictably yelled down, "I have to go to the bathroom. Can I go?"

I responded by bounding up the stairs and saying firmly, "Brett, you have been sent to your room because of your behavior. This is not when you get to go to the bathroom, get water, get food, play a game, rent a movie – whatever. You are to sit in here and think about what we talked about and why you are in trouble. Then I will come up and we will talk some more – then you can go to the bathroom."

Whining, "But Dad, I have to go really bad."

Firm, "I don't care – you can hold it for a few minutes." Maybe five minutes later I came upstairs. We talked, and I released him to freedom once more, taking the fact that he did not race off to the bathroom as confirmation that he really didn't need to go that badly.

Over the next few months, when Brett was sent to his room, he seemed to be taking his punishment better; we weren't hearing his constant requests to leave his room any longer. Unfortunately, this new behavior correlated with an increasing smell of urine in his room. Julie and I went through his room many times, checking his bed, looking in the closet, under his bed, in his dirty clothes hamper etc. and couldn't figure out where the smell was coming from. Julie was always airing the room out, and sometimes it wouldn't be so bad – but other times it would knock you off your feet.

After a few months, eventually something fell behind his tall dresser and Julie was on her hands and knees looking under it when the ammonia smell almost caused her to black out. We pulled back the dresser and came to the realization that when Brett was sent to his room, he had been peeing on the wall behind his dresser – apparently ever since I wouldn't let him go to the bathroom that one day. We had to have a section of drywall taken out and replace all the carpet around and under the dresser. It was gross.

I can't remember what we did to him, honestly. It was so surreal, that I think we all just moved forward. Clearly my oldest son was pissed about something. The behavior stopped with the discovery, and Brett recovered and took his place as a wonderful big brother to his younger siblings.

In addition to performance-based recovery, a second key selling point of the comfortable nest was that "You can ask us anything – and we mean anything – and we will give you the straight answer." This approach turned out to be useful for us in terms of having a sense of what the kids were being exposed to outside of the home. My kids have not held back on the questions, nor have we held back on the answers. Like the time thirteen-year-old Matthew asked me out of the blue, "Dad? What does oral sex mean?"

I tried to buy some time, "Ummm, Matthew, I have told you that you can ask me anything at all and I will give you the honest answer. So, I will tell you. But first, where did you hear this?"

Confidently, "SportsCenter."

"Really?"

Matthew replied, "Yeah. They said that Mike Tyson got out of prison today and he was in prison because he made this girl have oral sex with him and other stuff."

I mentally thanked Mike Tyson, as I would thank Bill Clinton a few years later, for helping me accelerate my kid's sex education pace. With President Clinton, it was my 10-year-old daughter Kelsey who asked the questions. She had heard something about cigars at school. Sweet.

My delay tactics had allowed me to gather my thoughts and I began, "Well, you already know that sex is between a man and a woman who are in love and that it involves their private parts, their sexual parts, coming together for the pleasurable purpose of showing their love to each other, and to have babies."

I wiped some sweat off my brow and continued, "You know all this, right? I mean, we have gone through this with the where babies come from discussion, right? Are we on the same page?" He is nodding.

I plow forward, "So oral sex is obviously a kind of sex. That means it is also going to involve a man's or a woman's private parts, their sexual parts, right?"

I get a guttural, "Uh huh."

"Okay. Now, you know in school when you give an oral presentation, what do you do?"

My son, "You give a speech."

"Right, you orate, or use your mouth to make the speech." I make the connection for him, "So oral sex involves those two things – the private parts and the mouth."

I was prepared to go further when I suddenly saw the light bulb go off in my son's head and he quietly said to me, "So Dad, like…a blow job?"

I stuttered, "Well, um, yes that is exactly what it is. Oral sex is just a more formal and broader name for that."

My son thinks for a few seconds and takes his next logical step, "So with a girl…"

I cut him off. "You know, I think that you probably get it now, and I trust you to fill in the rest. Okay?"

Clearly in the comfortable nest I was more at ease lecturing about the virtues of an open dialogue than I was actually answering some of the direct questions that resulted from my encouragement. Either way, I was lecturing, which I viewed as a large part of my job as Dad. I felt that way because of the way I had been raised. Since I am very close with my brother and sister and consider them to be wonderful people with good hearts and minds, I had evidence that my Dad's incessant lecturing, as painful as it often was, did absolutely nothing to screw up his kids. Accordingly, when Julie and I were having our hopes and dreams discussions, I knew that my best chance to be a decent father was to show up and follow Dad's template to the letter, which meant that I would use the lecture to impart all the important stuff. With this mindset, I actually felt prepared for a moment. I was ready to have a baby. A *baby?*

It was this last thought that stopped me in my tracks. For all my preparation in committing to show up, scrutinizing how my parents had built a comfortable nest, and developing my own lecture platform, I realized that I was now ready to be a Dad to like a 10-year-old. Unfortunately, I was about to have a *baby* in a week or so, not a 10-year-old. All my confidence went out the window and my worry gene kicked in as I remembered how pitiful I was with babies and realized that my plan of action did not address how to parent a newborn.

HAPPY HOLIDAYS FROM THE HENDERSONS

There is nothing I enjoy more than having some actual news to share with our family and friends when I sit down to write this letter each year. In the past two I really haven't had much to share with you since our lives didn't change too much from year to year. In 1987 things changed dramatically when, on August 1, we welcomed our daughter Kelsey Elizabeth to the family.

Brett (5) and Matthew (3 ½) are now big brothers and Julie and I are the proud parents of a baby girl. We are glad Kelsey was a girl because the Doctor has informed Julie that he will not go through another pregnancy with her after complications in the delivery room occurred for the second time in a row. The fact that we are now done having kids triggered a logical follow up conversation between Julie and I – "Who gets fixed so we really don't get pregnant again?"

To be honest, there wasn't much of a conversation here. Julie simply said, "You have seen me pump out three babies up close and personal. Now that we are done having kids, I think that you should get a vasectomy." As hard as I tried, I could not come up with a reasonable argument to her logic. It seemed the least I could do after not really contributing much in the delivery room over three births. The vasectomy procedure is another story for another day (probably not appropriate Christmas letter content) but I would like to think that Julie and I are even now. (THIS IS JULIE INSERTING A COMMENT: "NOT EVEN CLOSE.")

For the birth of Kelsey, I was more prepared than ever for the delivery room and I attribute my preparedness to the fact that we DIDN'T do Lamaze classes this time. Without the stress and pressure of Lamaze classes weighing on me, I handled this birth beautifully. I also did something I once thought I'd never do – I brought a video camera into the delivery room to record the event.

While recording the birth of our daughter was important to us, I had an ulterior motive for bringing in the video camera – I wanted to record the nurse's horrible treatment of me in the delivery room. I expected this after the way nurses treated me for both of the boy's births. Not surprisingly, the nurses were on best behavior with the tape running so all we have is the miracle of Kelsey's birth on tape - no "Nightline" footage of the nurses. Bummer.

Other than the birth of Kelsey, 1987 was similar to last year for our family – there were no big changes. I am still working at Jones Intercable and am truly enjoying my job and the people I work with. Julie is enjoying being a Mom more than ever – especially with another girl around the house. We both turned 30 this year. Brett and Matthew are busy boys who are enjoying being big brothers. We are blessed.

1987 will also be remembered as the year the Dow closed above 2,000 for the first time. I am thrilled about this since we finally joined the investing class a couple of years ago. Sometime in 1985 we actually had some money left over after paying all the bills, so I bought into a mutual fund. Saving – what a concept, let's hope it continues.

To our family and friends, we wish you the best of all things as we turn the page to 1988.

Merry Christmas and Happy New Year!

Love, Ted, Julie, Brett, Matthew and Kelsey

CHAPTER 3
THREE BABIES IN FIVE YEARS

Of all the things that I didn't see coming, and there have been many, my reaction to being the father of a newborn has to rank near the top. When I fantasized about being a Dad, I was always doing something active like playing ball, helping with schoolwork, proudly watching them in some activity, or teaching them about the important things in life. In other words, they were not babies in my fantasies. I knew this about babies - they sleep, cry, and mess their diapers. You have to feed them. I assumed the stage would be characterized as mostly maintenance and wondered, "How fun and exciting can that be?"

As the delivery date for our first approached I was worried that I wouldn't enjoy being a Dad to a newborn. I wasn't sure how I would react to them, or they to me. So far in my life all babies hated me and I made them cry. Panic was beginning to set in, even though I had semi-established a long-term parenting plan anchored by a commitment to show up.

Incredibly, the job of showing up became the easiest thing in the world when the kids were actually born. Words cannot explain what happened to me when I saw my children brought into the world. I fell so completely in love with these tiny babies that I didn't know what to do with myself. It strengthened my resolve to not screw this up – I was keenly aware that I was their father and knew that I held responsibility for their fragile, early lives literally in my hands. Whatever I thought was important before seemed to diminish in the face of being a Dad.

We had our three children over a five-year period and because I fell so hard for them, I became intimately involved and got very comfortable doing the all of the basic baby tasks from the get-go. Diapers, baths, rocking them to sleep, burping them, cleaning up their spit-up, walking around with one of them on my shoulder screaming and crying, taking them for walks in their strollers, sucking buggers out of their nose with the plunger thing etc. - all of this became part of my daily routine in relief of Julie. As long as I was with the babies, it didn't matter what it was, I was happy and loved it.

41

In a reversal of the effect I had on all other babies, I even established myself as the valuable go-to-guy when we needed to stop the child from crying. With all three of my babies, no matter what they were crying about, Daddy could always make it stop. Harking back to my hoop's days, I incessantly talked trash to my wife about my skills in this area. She tolerated the trash talk because the ends justified the means – the babies actually stopped crying!

In fairness, I have to give all the credit to Julie for the comfort level I achieved with our children when they were infants. A few days after we got home with Brett, she fed him and handed him to me and said, "I'm going to go out for a few hours. You stay here and take care of Brett. Have fun." No other instruction was given, and she just left. In hindsight this was probably the smartest thing she could have done. I was left alone with my newborn son and we bonded. My first diaper experience was a disaster, but it didn't matter, because I could do no wrong. This was because my wife was not there looking over my shoulder telling me what I was doing wrong. I became comfortable being a Dad to a newborn baby.

I probably loved the baby stage most of all because I could feel the unconditional love coming back at me so strongly from the little ones. From the moment their eyes could focus, and their hands could wrap around my pinky finger, I could see that my babies loved their Daddy. This, of course, made being a Dad the absolute coolest thing in the world. For me the key to being a decent parent was to be there from the very start, when they arrived as babies, and that unconditional love thing grabbed me by the throat. It was quite easy to show up thereafter.

I was in the delivery room for the birth of all three of our children, barely for the first one. Most first baby stories include something like an 18-hour labor in the hospital and finally a delivery. This is the case more often than not as the new parents arrive at the hospital at the first sign of labor and then end up waiting and waiting and waiting. Not us. The reason? My wife's obstetrician had told her that there would be no question when she went into labor. It would rank among the most severe pains she had ever experienced and it would be unmistakable. Unfortunately, the doctor didn't realize what a high tolerance for pain my wife has — I mean, she married me.

So, on the morning of July 14, 1982, I woke up and found my wife in pretty severe pain. I also noticed that the pain was coming and going, like every 20 minutes or so. Things seemed pretty clear to me, we were going to have a baby today. I was excited, and it was a work day, so I said, "This is it. I will call work and let them know I'm not going to make it in today."

Grunting through obvious pain, my wife said to me, "No. You go in to work. This isn't it yet."

Stunned, I said, "Huh? Umm, what do you think this is?"

"I don't know, but it isn't unbearably painful, so it can't be the real thing. Honestly honey, you go into work. This will pass, and if it doesn't, I will call you and then we will go in."

She turned and went into the bathroom. Listening through the door it sounded to me like she was trying to have our first child in the toilet. I gently asked again, "Honey, are you sure that I should leave? I mean everyone knows we are close to having a baby. It won't be a big deal if I stay home with you even if it is a false alarm."

She responded, "Please go in to work. I will be fine. This seems to be passing now that I am sitting down. I am much more comfortable in here."

Pondering her insistence, I concluded that she had to know more about this than I did. I mean all the real serious stuff was happening *inside her.* I know that I would make no mistakes about something that was happening inside of my body. I assumed she knew more about her body than I did, so I prepared to leave for work and I said through the closed bathroom door, "You know that if you have the baby in the toilet, boy or girl we are naming it John."

She didn't appreciate my humor as she was starting what we would soon find out was another contraction, now about nineteen minutes apart. Clueless, I went off to work on the audit of a cable television company, about a fifteen-minute drive away. When I arrived at work my phone rang immediately and it was of course Julie. "Honey" was all she got out when she dropped the phone in pain. I listened to her grunt and moan for about a minute and then she came back on line. "Ted. Come home quick. I am in labor and we need to get to the hospital fast."

Bummed that I did not even get a chance to say, "I told you so", I ran to my car and raced home to find my wife on the floor in the bathroom fighting another contraction. I said, "Are you okay?"

The contraction ended, and she spoke haltingly, "Get me to the hospital. The doctor said I am definitely in labor – and close."

I moved to help her off the floor saying, "Let me help you to the car and then I'll get the Lamaze bag."

She said, "Screw the Lamaze bag. Get me to the hospital."

I stopped in my tracks and repeated in my head, "Screw the Lamaze bag? *Screw the Lamaze bag!*" Wow, I thought, this must be really serious.

The Lamaze bag had been the bane of my existence for the past few months. My pregnant (read: crazy) wife viewed Lamaze as critical to doing pregnancy and delivery the right way. Predictably I didn't take it as seriously as she did, and I made fun of it as often as possible. In my defense, I was taking this all very seriously, as I think you can see. However, I thought Lamaze was a bit of a crock and I didn't hesitate to make fun of it, which annoyed Julie tremendously.

I would like to know how a husband is supposed to react (other than with some humor) when he finds out during Lamaze class that there is a vaginal exercise called Kegels - and that are 10 different levels of vaginal contractions *before* the woman reaches a level the Lamaze instructors called 'the basement.' Julie was mortified when I asked the Lamaze instructor, "Is basement the level at which a wife can literally tear her husband's penis off his body?" The husbands in the class thought this was a funny question while all the wives, including Julie, seemed to hate me.

44

In my defense, I got the main point of Lamaze after the first five minutes of the first class. "Breathe when it hurts." Okay, I got it. Seems logical, since it has worked for centuries. Breathe when it hurts, we got it. I don't need any more classes where you pretend I am really involved in this and you call me Coach. I certainly don't need anymore Kegel intimidation.

Even after the classes mercifully ended, I continued to make fun of the Lamaze bag that we were to prepare for the trip to the hospital. I had recently commented that the contents suggested for the Lamaze bag seemed more appropriate for survival after a nuclear event than for a brief hospital stay. I honestly think I could have survived in the wilderness for a month on the bags suggested contents, and I am no Jeremiah Johnson. It seemed like overkill to me.

My wife, however, was sold hook, line and sinker on the gospel according to the Lamaze instructors. "Ted, this is important. Don't forget the Lamaze bag. Please, this is the one job I am asking you to do." Now that game time was here, she had finally arrived at the same conclusion I had reached after the first Lamaze class - "Screw the Lamaze bag".

The fact that she agreed with me on anything made me think that we must be really close to having a baby. I thought, "I might have to deliver this baby on the way to the hospital." I looked around and grabbed a blanket and my softball mitt, figuring I might have to catch a baby shooting out of my wife while doing 70 mph on the Interstate. I remember thinking confidently, "I can do that. I'll make the grab. I am about to be Dad."

The hospital, St. Josephs in Denver where all three of our children were born, was about a half hour drive away and we made it in twenty minutes. Arthur Andersen & Company (my employer at the time) did the audit of the hospital and when we arrived I ran into two of my buddies from work near the ER entrance. I acted like I was totally on top of things and started talking with them, ignoring my wife who was being helped into a wheel chair by nurses and hospital attendants. She had another contraction and writhed in pain. My friends said, "Umm, Ted. You might want to help Julie."

I turned to follow behind a nurse who was pushing Julie's wheelchair into the hospital. I had noticed that this nurse had been glaring at me while I was speaking with my friends. Maybe I over read things, but her look sent a clear message: "I don't like you. You are not ready to be a father." As she was wheeling Julie in, she looked over her shoulder at me and said in a cool tone, "So sir, why didn't you get her here earlier? This is your first baby, right?"

I replied tentatively, "Yes, it is. And I tried to get her here earlier, I really did. But then I went to work and…"

She jumped in and cut me off, "You went to work? Sir, your wife's contractions are about three minutes apart here. You are going to have a baby in about 15 minutes. Didn't you take Lamaze classes?" I nodded. "Well then you know this is your job. You should be the one thinking straight here. She is clearly in labor. What were you thinking going into work with her in this condition? C'mon Coach."

Calling me Coach stirred memories of the classes I had loathed and all I could think was, man, do I hate that **** Lamaze. I stammered, "Well, I …I guess I wasn't thinking."

The nurse convicted me, "No, you weren't." To my wife, "It's okay honey. You are in good hands with us now." The implication was clear - I sucked as a husband and would probably suck as a Dad.

This was the first of what would be a series of three bad nurse experiences for me, all related to my being a Dad. I admit that I have been uncomfortable around nurses ever since I was a kid since I still associate them with needles. I have luckily managed to avoid them for most of my life, but having babies is a sure way to encounter a nurse. This one seemed genuinely angry at me, and probably deservedly so. I knew I was clueless, and hated her for underscoring the fact.

Moving beyond our conflict the nurse wheeled Julie into the prep room. The doctor came in and examined my wife while I stood directly behind him. The gloved hand took inventory and he said excitedly, "Whoa there. You are a full 10 centimeters right now

46

Julie!" He looked from Julie to me and back to Julie. "You're going to have a baby here shortly!" To the nurses, "Let's get her in right away, she is crowning."

I heard all of this as background noise because, as I stood behind him and looked over his shoulder, I couldn't take my eyes off of what '10 centimeters' looked like. I believe that I have slipped into tighter parking spaces than that. I stayed tough and didn't black out, even though the nurse who hated me was openly taking bets that 'the sorry ass father would faint.'

When all was said and done, the birth went fine. Mom and child were fine. Our world had changed forever after the miracle of Brett's birth. For me this was the first of three life changing experiences I would witness over a five-year period that would define my life for the next twenty-five years. I would point out that we did virtually everything wrong in having our first baby, and everything still turned out okay. Looking back, I believe that having my softball mitt with me was far more important than Lamaze training.

Regardless of my views, for the birth of middle child Matthew, we again prepared as if for the invasion of Normandy and Lamaze was still at the core of the battle plan. We were going to re-learn everything again because we were going to re-take the classes *again*. I thought this was completely nuts as our first two babies were only going to come about 18 months apart. I was out voted and again had to endure hearing about Kegel levels and Lamaze bags all over again.

For Matthew's birth on February 29, 1984, we had more time at the hospital and I kept the Lamaze bag with me the entire time we were there. Beyond snack food, the Lamaze bag also contained all the things that were supposed to distract Julie from the incredible pain she was in. As part of my Coaching duties, I kept arbitrarily offering her stuff from the bag we had spent hours preparing and her response was either "No thanks", or a pained and guttural "Arghrghrarghra." Whenever I got the second response, I took this as a signal that I should help her breathe through the contraction like the good Coach I was trying to be.

47

"Breathe with me. C'mon honey. You are doing great, breathe. Oh yeah, nice. Come on good short breaths. Focal point! Focal point! Oh, that is fabulous. You are doing great. Breathe. Yes, that was a beautiful breath, that one there. Good, now breathe again. Throw a Kegel in their honey! Atta girl. Oh yeah. There you go. Perfect. Short breaths, come on. Now take that big cleansing breath. Beautiful. And we are done."

I thought two things. First, I thought, "Magnificent job, Coach." Second thing was, "Wow! Julie's breath is horrible!" She had thrown up dinner, a salad with extra bleu cheese dressing, about fifteen minutes prior. Brutal.

In that moment, I felt like the Wooden of the delivery room but as I looked up from what I thought was a masterful coaching job, I saw a nurse who looked exactly like Dick Butkus looking at me and shaking her head. What!? I had done nothing to this woman. I had arrived way early this time and was playing the role of Lamaze Coach reasonably well. I wasn't even watching television. Why was she staring at me and shaking her head as if I sucked?

When Julie's next contraction started, I began to help again, when Butkus said loudly from across the bed, "Look at me this time honey." My wife moved her focus from me to her and they breathed together for the entire contraction, almost exactly as I had.

When the contraction ended, my wife lay back on the bed and closed her eyes, completely spent and said to the nurse, "Thank you."

Butkus looked at me from across the bed, after checking to see if Julie's eyes were closed and mouthed, "You suck. I hate you. You should die."

Okay, I'm exaggerating – but just a bit. I had been replaced as Coach in the middle of the game by this nurse. I was pissed, but this quickly passed as I enjoyed watching the nurse's reaction to Julie's breath for the next hour. I happily told her that I had already chewed all the gum in the Lamaze bag, and there was none left for Julie. "Sorry Butkus".

Before being shoved out of the way, I had used down time between contractions to peruse the Lamaze bag for something that would help me contribute to the process. I could find nothing that would help among the unbelievable array of products contained in the bag. What the rolled-up tennis balls in the sock was all about was a complete mystery to me, so I banged it on my head a few times and then replaced it. There was lots of snack food, although the inventory was declining as I continued to eat. There was some lip balm. Four ball point pens. Scissors, crayons, and silly putty. A flare. $200 in cash. There was a parachute and a map of the United States. I wondered "Who is having this baby, D.B. Cooper?" I was reassured that Lamaze is definitely overkill. I ate some more stuff and pondered the parachute wondering if Julie had developed an escape plan from me that she hadn't shared.

About an hour later, Julie knocked me from a daydream and asked for a snack from the Lamaze bag. I had to come clean. There was nothing left to eat in the bag, and I was full. In my defense, for the last hour or so there wasn't anything for me to do but eat stuff out of the Lamaze bag and watch television. Butkus had made me obsolete, and I was scared of both her and Julie.

I wasn't involved again until I moved behind the doctor to witness the birth of my second child – another miracle. Julie's blood pressure suddenly went off the charts and there were a few scary minutes following the birth, where I was again pushed out of the way by nurses who helped my wife and hated me. My total involvement in this second birth was exactly the same as the first: I stood around and did nothing until they told me to come around and watch the episiotomy and the birth. Both times I wondered, couldn't you have called me over just after the episiotomy?

I want to point out that seeing your child come into the world is an amazing experience and I would never diminish its importance. However, the cynic in me believes that Dads are invited into the delivery room for another, more insidious reason. I believe we are encouraged to be there so we can actually see what happens to your wife's body when the baby is delivered. Having the Dad watch the actual birthing process really slants the tables in the wife's favor for the upcoming "Who gets fixed?" discussion that inevitably follows the birth of your last child.

For us there was no real discussion as Julie simply said to me, "I think you should get a vasectomy since I delivered the children. That seems fair, don't you think? Unless you are ready to pass a watermelon through your nose, this would seem to be the best thing you can do to level the playing field for us on the baby deliveries."

Honestly, how was I to argue this? I had seen three babies come out of my wife, and if it wasn't for the video of the third, I still wouldn't believe how it actually happens. I had seen two episiotomies, luckily missing the third as I decided against the Tarantino video version of Kelsey's birth. My wife's health was in question after delivering her second and third babies. After we had our third, her obstetrician said to her, "I'm glad we got you a girl this time, because I think you are done having babies from a health standpoint."

For once in my life I read a situation correctly and easily responded to her suggestion with, "No problem. Of course, I will get a vasectomy." The look on my wife's face told me that I had done something really great in volunteering. I know this because I have only seen that look four times in 27 years. Thankfully I shut up and didn't argue my case and ruin the moment by making the obvious point that the deliveries had been pretty tough on me too, you know with the pressure of being a Lamaze Coach and all.

Although the vasectomy remains a distant second to child bearing in terms of procedures that mess with your naughty parts, it is still a daunting experience that I tried to be macho about to impress my wife. I held that demeanor until the night before the procedure, when Julie got a call from the doctor's office while I was out at a business dinner. They gave her some vague instructions about my preparation for surgery and she passed them on to me when I got home. I read her notes and came to the following, "Shave your private area."

I pointed to it and said to Julie, "What does this mean?"

She said, "It means shave your private area."

I pressed, "Like a Yul Brunner type of shave, or something much less than that. What exactly did she say to you?"

"She said 'Your husband should make sure to shave his private area before he comes in for surgery'."

Ouch. This was the first time in a while that I was reminded that the vasectomy was a surgery. That word brings chills to me because it always involves nurses. The macho armor had been nicked significantly, so I lashed out at my wife. "And you didn't ask her to clarify 'shave your private area'? I bet if she told you to shave your private area you would say, 'How much exactly should I shave?' Brazilian? Kojak? How much? Don't you think?"

She popped back, "Well, I didn't. So, go with your gut. My guess would be to shave your testicles."

I physically jumped back, "My balls! Why would I do that?"

Smugly she replied, "Well, and this is just a wild guess, but because that is where the vas deferens are."

"Are you telling me that they are going to go straight in through my balls to do this?"

"I don't know for sure, but that would be my guess on *Jeopardy*." After a pause, "Honey, you don't look too good."

I had actually begun to sweat. There was no chance of backing out now, but I hadn't signed up for this, not in my mind. This felt like being on a ride at the amusement park that you really don't want to be on any more. I was in absolutely no condition to shave my private area. However, I had to get up and have a vasectomy in the morning, so I went upstairs and gave it a shot.

As I contemplated how to start, I just couldn't come to grips with my wife's interpretation. I thought, "That can't be right. There is hardly any hair there. They would have said 'shave your testicles' if that is what I was supposed to do. They must plan to come in from up here and have gravity on their side and work their way down to the target area." So, I attacked the hairier northern region and I worked on both sides rather aggressively. I started with scissors and then used a razor, and the final unfortunate result looked a lot like Mr. T with a long nose.

My wife took one look and burst out laughing. "Well, that's one way to interpret 'shave your private area'. You should do landscaping at Disney World. I'm still saying you should have shaved your testicles. I guess we'll find out tomorrow morning."

I started off on a bad note when I arrived at the doctor's office at 8:55 am. I was supposed to be there at 8:30 am and the nurses in the office were not happy with me. Of all the surgeries where you don't want to have doctors and nurses angry with you, the vasectomy has to rank at the top.

After a rushed registration I was hurried into a side office for a conference with the doctor, but I don't remember much after I heard the words "injection" and "incision" and how those words were being applied to my balls. I hated to admit it, but Julie was right about the target area and I was not even close. I was a bit self conscious about the way my landscaped private area looked based on the pre-surgery discussion and I hoped that the doctor would be the only one to see me naked. After the pre-game conference where I signed away any reservations about this being hard to reverse, I was taken to the room where the surgery would be performed, and I soon found myself in stirrups, with nothing but a towel guarding my naked lower half. I was alone with an attractive, but angry nurse. I was terrified.

She unceremoniously whipped off my towel, stared for a moment at my private area and said, "That's not right."

I responded sheepishly, "I didn't get very clear instructions about where to shave."

"Obviously. Well, I'll show you." She proceeded to lather up my balls and shave them.

I was sporting about a half-inch of manhood at this point as my guy tried to hide in what was left of the bushes. I was bursting to say, in my best Mr. T voice, "I pity the fool who be shaving my balls!", but I don't think the nurse would have gotten the Mr. T reference. She finished shaving me and appraised her handiwork. As she moved away, I clearly saw a smug, "What an average penis" look on her face.

I wanted to jump at her and say, "Hey, lady! You get that average penis look off your face right now. My guy is in hiding, drawing up like a turtle because the Doc over there has just openly said he is going straight through my balls with an injection and an incision and then he is going to snip something, and I don't remember what all else. You might as well judge me in a pool of ice water."

The doctor came in at that moment and seemed all excited to get going, which he did. I didn't like the vasectomy procedure one bit, especially when the doctor "lost an end" and dug rather aggressively somewhere way up inside me to find it. Finally, we were done. The post-op instructions from the doctor included the following: "Remember that you have to clean the pipes, or you will risk becoming pregnant. Come back in a week, after you have had around 10 ejaculations and we will test you to make sure you are clear."

As a father of three, I'm thinking, "Ten ejaculations in a week? What are you, a porn star?"

Julie drove me home and I told her (expectantly) what the doctor had said. She said (dismissively), "It sounds like it is off to the showers for the big left hander." I retired to the couch with a lawn bag full of ice covering my lower half. I was numb from my bellybutton to my knees and I sat that way for three days and didn't move or eat. It is now about 20 years later, and I have used up all my vasectomy points and am back on "no credit" with Julie.

I don't care though because before the nightmare that was my vasectomy, there was August 1, 1987, the day I became the father of a baby girl at the age of 30. When Kelsey was born, I was struck by how different the notion of a baby girl felt after having two boys. I believed that I knew how to raise boys, at least so far at 5 and 3 ½, I felt I hadn't screwed up too badly. A girl was going to be a whole

53

new experience. I worried and thought, "What if she is as crazy as her Mom?" Before we even left the delivery room, the reality of having a daughter strummed a discordant note on my worry guitar and the hair on the back of my neck rose. Was I ready to be the father of a baby girl? It just felt different. I soon found out that it was.

I realized early that daddy/daughter relationships are special. From the moment she was born, Kelsey owned me and everyone in the family knew it. She is probably the child who is most like me, which means it is amazing my wife has survived us both. Among my three kids, I admit that my daughter was by far the most spoiled and that has created some self-inflicted parenting challenges. There are reasons why Kelsey was indulged more than the boys that go beyond the fact that she was our only girl and the baby in the family. In addition to these facts, at the age of 3, Kelsey had her first seizure and was later diagnosed with epilepsy.

Long-term health issues with your baby girl will serve to take some parenting bite out of the best laid disciplinary plans and although we were determined not to let epilepsy define her life, because of the frequency of her seizures, it became the elephant in the room. So, Daddy spoiled his little girl just a bit. Kelsey has been on about a dozen medications over the past sixteen years with varying success. The best year while on meds was when she had only ten seizures; the worst was when she had over three hundred. Without meds, she usually has at least one a day.

Luckily, her seizures have been generally confined to her sleep cycle and because of this she has lived a relatively normal life. Spending a lot of time at Children's Hospital brought perspective to us and Kelsey realized that what she was dealing with paled in comparison to what many other children were coping with. This didn't eliminate the fact that she was handling some heavy stuff, it just brought perspective to her which has helped her navigate the waters she was in.

As I write this, we are planning to go to the Mayo Clinic in May 2007 to see if Kelsey is a surgery candidate. There are still many hurdles to go through before she is considered a candidate and even then, the odds are only 50% that they can eliminate her seizures completely.

Kelsey seems determined to go down this path and we are hopeful for her. She recently told me "Daddy, I don't want to be 30 years old and wonder why I didn't try everything possible to eliminate my seizures. I want to try the surgery thing if I am a candidate." Of all the things I have faced being a Dad, the uncertainty and lack of control over the epilepsy issue ranks as the most frustrating – our first true bump in the road as a family.

When Kelsey was born, my wife and I had just turned 30 years old. Although we had plenty of energy, we did not fully understand the journey that was still ahead of us. I blindly launched a plan that began what I called the foundation lectures and hoped things would turn out okay.

HAPPY HOLIDAYS FROM THE HENDERSONS

I wish that I had some compelling, incredibly upbeat news that would lift everyone's spirits at holiday time this year, but alas, I don't. 1991 has been a year for our family - not a great year, not a lousy year...another year. With Brett (9) in 4th grade, Matthew (7) in 2nd grade, and Kelsey (4) in pre-school, we're dealing with three basic sociopaths (I mean that in the nicest holiday way) whose main goal in life seems to be to drive Julie and I to the nuthouse.

While the sociopath description may be a bit overstated, I point out that if you look up the definition in Webster's, a sociopath is a person whose behavior lacks a sense of moral responsibility or social conscience. Honestly, that seems to define our kids...if they were left to their own devices which, luckily, they are not.

Julie and I continue to work hard to try to build a solid foundation under the kids where they establish some balance in their lives and develop a sense of responsibility and accountability towards others. Once they get this, we expect them to leave the comfortable nest of home and live their independent lives on their own nickel. I can't really tell how things are going yet – check back with me in about 15 years.

Julie and I celebrated our 12th anniversary this year. She deserves better, but I've somehow convinced her that my lack of maturity and discipline are endearing traits if you look at them with a glass is half full attitude. She is a fabulous mother who is involved in all aspects of the children's lives. I am basically responsible for maintaining gainful employment which, to the surprise of anyone who really knows me, I've done. This marks the end of my 8th year at Jones Intercable.

I am also the coach for many of the kid's youth sports teams in soccer, baseball, T-Ball, and basketball. In a EUREKA moment, I have figured out the answer to soccer's problems in becoming a major sport in the U.S. While coaching Brett and Matthew in soccer over the last few years, I realized that the games are much better when the rules stipulate "NO GOALIES". With no goalies, I coached in games that finished 12 – 10. Exciting! As soon as Brett was old enough to start playing with goalies, the score of every game has been 0 – 0; the same score of every real soccer game I have seen throughout my life. Not exciting! Sorry, but without allowing the talented athletes to score once in a while, soccer will never take off in this country. Eliminating goalies is definitely the answer. You are welcome, FIFA.

While 1991 was just another relatively quiet year for the Henderson's, there was plenty of stuff in the national news to comment on, although none of it was too inspiring either. On the good news front, the Gulf War came and went almost overnight as we pushed Saddam back into Iraq quickly...and then we inexplicably stopped. I'm sure we have not heard the last from that guy.

Elsewhere, the news was even less inspiring. Magic Johnson announced that he has HIV; William Kennedy Smith proudly followed in his Uncle Teddy's footsteps; the Clarence Thomas confirmation hearings were a joke as Democrats (including the aforementioned Ted Kennedy) hammered away at a very qualified man over nothing; and Rodney King, the new voice of the people, asked everyone to "Just get along." Do we live in a great country or what? I wish I had videotape of how the nurses treated me in the delivery room for Brett and Matthew's birth. Maybe now I'd be a pseudo celebrity like Rodney King.

(THIS IS JULIE INSERTING A COMMENT: "TED - NO ONE CARES ABOUT THIS STUFF. THIS IS SUPPOSED TO BE A CHRISTMAS LETTER. SHARE SOMETHING ABOUT THE FAMILY PLEASE.")

Honestly, it is hard to share something interesting about the family every twelve months because things just don't change that much year to year. We are blocking and tackling. I know others share compelling family stuff every year, convincing us that they are making the world a better place, but I am assuming that you are just not that interested in the intimate details of our lives. Julie wants me to tell you about what we did to the backyard this summer or about our spring vacation. Come on – you guys enjoy my rambling commentary more than you would enjoy that, right?

We truly wish our friends and family members a wonderful holiday season and may God bless all of you as 1992 approaches.

Love, Ted, Julie, Brett, Matthew and Kelsey

CHAPTER 4
THE FOUNDATION LECTURES

Among Dad's Top Ten Lectures, I viewed the first four as the most important. To this day, I still talk about the foundation building basics to my adult children when appropriate circumstances (in my mind, never theirs) arise. They often stop me before I can get started because they have heard it all before and know all the points that I am about to make. I like that they know the basics, but they are still going to hear from me. My 82-year-old Dad still gives me a periodic foundation lecture to lend perspective when I have lost some, and I am comforted when he does.

I admit that I pushed the issue on the foundation lectures with the kids just a bit. Remember, I was trying to be a good Dad and overachievement was my calling card. Julie caught me lecturing Brett one night and said, "Honey, he is 18 months old. I don't think he understands what you are saying."

To which I responded, "There is no harm in starting to build a solid foundation right now. Brett will never find it unusual that his Dad is talking common sense to him because he will never know anything different. It is what he will expect. Seriously, how much harm can there be in talking about the basics to an 18-month-old?"

This was one of the few battles that I won in our marriage, so I started these lectures almost the moment the kids arrived. Of course, the kids didn't know they were getting foundation lectures. They just knew that a guy called Daddy loved them very much and seemed to always be there with something to say to them. The fact that they knew and trusted this early in their lives, I knew from experience, was the start of building a strong foundation.

FOUNDATION LECTURE # 1
FAITH

I want to make it clear that in leading off the foundation lectures with faith I am not holding myself out to be any type of Christian role model. To provide some scale, I figure that if the Pope and Mother Theresa are A + rated on the Christian continuum, I probably come in at a solid D. Barely passing, but enough to save me. While I do not view myself as a Christian role model, I am proud of my faith and happy to live in a country where Judeo/Christian values are held by over 80% of the population.

Like millions of others, Julie and I both grew up in Christian homes and have always considered our faith to be a defining part of who we are. So, faith was a foundation lecture not just because we believed in everlasting salvation, but also because the tenets of the Christian faith provided good basic rules for young children trying to find their way in the world. "No killing, no stealing, no lying, and no cheating. Treat people the way you would like to be treated. Be respectful of others, be humble, be trustworthy, and be compassionate. Work hard and trust that your life here has a purpose." The backdrop of faith allowed us to define an expected moral code of conduct for the kids which would hopefully lead to a strong set of core values.

I knew that the ultimate strength of their Christian faith would be a personal journey over which Julie and I had little control. As a young parent in my mid-twenties, I understood that much of what our children learned about faith inside of the home and inside the church would be challenged on the outside. I knew that they would inevitably confront and re-examine their beliefs as they got older, the same way I had. The fact that I was raised with tremendous (self-imposed) guilt in the Catholic Church almost guaranteed that I was going to re-examine my beliefs later in life. The spark that fueled the confronting of my beliefs was getting married and preparing to have children - I started to do some broader reading on the subjects of faith and evolution outside of the Catholic Church for the first time in my early twenties.

Through my reading early in our married life, I knew that I was much more aligned with the views of C.S. Lewis than those of Darwin or Freud. Reading Lewis's *Mere Christianity* was a defining moment for me. For the first time I looked at my faith not through the prism of Catholicism but as, well... mere Christianity. On the broader intelligent design front, I simply could not come to grips with a view that held that everything I saw was some evolutionary bit of good luck and that our short life here on earth had no meaning or purpose.

To me, it took an even greater leap of faith to assume no one was at the controls.

As an adult, I have questioned, prayed, and studied my faith in an effort to strengthen it or dismiss it. It has only grown stronger as I have matured, and I am comfortable in my own skin as a Christian now; but Catholic childhood guilt dies hard – like never. As healthy as I believe a bit of guilt can be at times, it was the one thing about my faith that I didn't want to pass on to the kids.

I told the kids that despite my personal struggles with the church I was raised in, faith has been the part of my personal foundation that I have most frequently leaned upon. I can think of nothing that has been more important in my life. So, within the home of a Christian Dad unlikely to have many stars in his crown in heaven, faith easily won the number one spot in Dad's Top Ten Lectures; it was the anchor of the foundation lectures. Off of this broad topic, I could go almost anywhere. Building and maintaining a solid moral character, becoming a caring and compassionate human being, having a commitment to family, atoning for questionable behavior, being accountable, understanding unconditional love – I could credibly tie all of these (important) topics to lectures that started with the basic premise of faith.

When the deeper question of heaven and hell came up, the faith lecture moved from developing a solid moral code to the ultimate pass/fail test. I faced the inevitable question from the kids as they got older and their scope of friends increased. "Dad, so do you believe that all Jewish people, or Muslims, or Mormons, you know who don't believe Christ is the Son of God…do you believe they will never go to heaven?"

I answered them honestly, if not biblically, in the way I had internally resolved this question for myself years earlier. "I think that the way we live our life on earth matters. As a Christian, I believe that Christ is the Son of God and I believe that accepting that fact is the only way to get to heaven. However, I also believe that Christ has a way to show himself to non-Christians who otherwise live what we would consider to be a Christian type of life. Maybe these people didn't ever have an opportunity to hear about Christ's love or maybe they were raised in a home that worshipped a different God. I believe there is a place for these children of God in heaven; that Christ somehow reveals the truth to them. Maybe that happens on their death bed, you know, maybe that tunnel of light that you hear about. I don't know. But no, I don't think it is as simple as all Christians go to heaven and all others go to hell. I think there is more to it than that. I struggle with the notion that Gandhi is burning in hell."

I don't know if this was the right answer to give to the kids, again, certainly it wasn't biblically based. I knew that they would inevitably confront their faith as adults and they could come to their own conclusions about this tough question later in life. For now, I felt it was a better answer for a ten-year-old kid confronting the mysteries of faith than, "Yeah, that is a tough one. I'm sorry, but these four friends of yours are definitely toast."

Beyond lectures to the kids anchored by faith, I have to admit that I was not above using faith in the comfortable nest to try to get out of the doghouse with Julie. When I was in a bit of trouble with her the blessing, I gave at dinner might go something like this, "Dear Lord, thank you so much for this day. Thank you for the many blessings you have bestowed upon our family. Thank you for Mom and her efforts to prepare this wonderful meal for us." I'd pause and then continue. "And Lord, please help Mom find it in her heart to forgive Dad. We pray that Mom can accept Dad back into her arms the same way she would accept a sickly, stray animal that has lost his way. We hope that she can do this right now so that dinner will not be uncomfortable for the children. In your heavenly name we pray, amen."

The kid's always thought this was funny and immediately started asking questions like, "What did you do now, Dad?" and the dialogue that followed would usually help my case. Eventually one of the kids would say, "That doesn't seem like such a big deal to me."

To which I would respond, "Me either," and then look at Julie.

Since it was just after dinnertime prayers, she was unlikely to make a big deal about things, so she would laugh and generally let whatever it was go. At least until we were alone again. At that point I would hear the following, "I hate it when you bring up an issue you and I are having in front of the kids. It just isn't fair."

And I would respond, "I was just praying that you would find it in your heart to forgive me. It is important for the kids to see that prayers are sometimes answered. Just think, if you are nice to me, we can tell the kid's that they have witnessed a miracle."

FOUNDATION LECTURE #2
BALANCED LIFE

The premise for this sermon was simple and straightforward: "Anybody can focus on one thing and do it well. However, to truly enjoy life you need to have more than one thing going for you – you need some balance." To communicate this to my children, I had to do two things: (1) define what made up a balanced life and (2) pass it on to them in a way that they could remember.

My Dad had done this for me when I was younger, and he was working on building my foundation. I was going through a tough time with something as a teenager and he was explaining to me that bumps in the road of life were inevitable and balance was required to navigate the unavoidable hurdles successfully. He used his hand as a visual aid to make his point and I remembered it so, as with most of my parenting efforts, I stole the balanced life lecture and the visual accompaniment directly from my Dad.

When talking to my kids I would spread out my hand with all five fingers extended, bobbing up and down as if floating on a roiling sea and begin. "Each finger on my hand represents a specific area of interest or focus in what would be defined as a well-balanced life." I wiggled each finger starting with the thumb as I named the five balanced life categories. "Faith, family, friends, work and play. This is a life that is in balance and has a lot going for it. It can survive on the ever-changing sea of life because balance provides ballast – that means you can float. It is hard to defeat or sink a well-balanced life. If something awful happens, let's say Daddy loses his job, the work part of my balanced life is going to suffer for awhile."

I deflate the ring finger representing work and still have four fingers extended strongly. "While the work area of my life suffers during this time, faith (wiggle the thumb), family (wiggle the index finger), friends (wiggle the middle finger), and play (wiggle the pinky) are all still there to help me get through the tough times and move on with my life. All my eggs are not in one basket. You see what I am saying here? Are you guys with me on this?" Nods indicate that they get it, but I always checked.

"So, if the completely spread out hand represents balance that can help you float on the bumpy sea of life," I wiggle all the extended fingers repeating the categories again and move my hand in a gentle floating motion, "then the closed fist is a rock, a life with no balance that is destined to sink. If you only have one thing going for you (I extend one finger) and that one thing takes a hit (I close the one finger) your life drops like a rock." I dropped the closed fist to illustrate my point. "If you have balance," I start to re-inflate the fingers and lift the floating hand repeating faith, family, friends, work and play, "you can get through the tough times and stay afloat."

I was obviously anal about my delivery of this lecture. In my mind I needed to be convincing since the balanced life lecture was frequently given when something lousy was happening in a specific area of one of my children's lives. I was often soothing a hurt child when giving this foundation lecture because one part of their life had probably taken a hit and they needed to be reminded that they had a lot more going for them than just the one thing. As you can imagine, with three kids, I gave this lecture quite a bit.

I viewed the inclusion of faith in a balanced life as reinforcement for what they already knew from the first foundation lecture. The family part of the balanced life lecture frequently melted into the comfortable nest concept and vice versa. Family was a relatively easy sell since Mom and I had been there for the kids since the day they were born and were a constant in their young lives. A similar family constant was their sibling relationships, which were important to the kids, and they nurtured them naturally.

As I knew from my own life, after faith and family, friends were the other leg of the stool that helped keep me accountable and made life worth living. I've been lucky and blessed to have good friends throughout my life who have helped me in more ways than they will ever know. As I have gotten older and maintained many of my childhood and young adult friendships, I love looking back with an adult sense of clarity as to why I choose these people as my friends when I was younger and why, when we get together as adults, it is as if no time at all has passed – we simply pick up where were and enjoy our time together as lifelong friends.

I knew that I would do well as a parent to recognize this simple fact - the friends that my children chose in elementary school and beyond would have a significant impact on their lives. Accordingly, Julie and I did everything we could to get to know who our kids were hanging out with. Like faith and family, good friends held a critical position in the balanced life, and the three combined to help establish accountability to others beyond the individual. Without a solid base including the three "F's", work and play wouldn't matter too much.

Like the way the three "F's" were connected in a balanced life, so were work and play. The work category represented productivity, but it didn't usually involve choice. Ultimately work meant a real job, and I was quick to point out the importance (and the monetary impact) of work. "The good news is that you get paid for doing work. Getting paid is an extremely important part of being an independent adult – it allows you to eat and put a roof over your head, two great motivators. You will work and be productive for most of your adult life and enjoy the fruits of your labor. What you do for work is a critical part of a well-balanced life."

The play category played counterpoint to work because choice was involved. I knew that play was a critical part of their young lives and I wanted them to understand that Dad still played, even in his thirties and forties. Play time was free time, although it was connected to work and was just as important a part of the balanced life. I made sure the kids learned that within the balanced life, they earned play through work.

The balanced life lecture was all about the big picture. It was the lecture that served as shorthand for what my Dad still says to me to this day: "When you are feeling sorry for yourself, make a two-column list. In one column, list everything that you have going on in your life that's positive. In the other column list everything that is going on in your life that's negative. Now, compare the columns. Life isn't really so bad, is it?"

As Dad, I wanted to make sure that my kids could easily access this thought process and the "hand lecture" was my weapon. Generally, the balanced life lecture was meant to be an encouragement that they were approaching life the right way, they had a lot going for them, and they were on track to lead a successful life, however they chose to define it.

FOUNDATION LECTURE #3
WITH EVERY RIGHT COMES RESPONSIBILITY

I wanted this foundation concept to become a part of my children's DNA because I knew that, outside of the comfortable nest, they would be exposed to a substantial discussion about their rights and a not so substantial discussion about their responsibilities. I believed that a one-sided view of rights without a balancing of responsibility would inevitably lead to an "I am owed" mentality that could damage a productive mindset. So, I drove this point home with a passion. Because this lecture was almost always a short monologue, it was probably the most frequently delivered among Dad's Top Ten.

While delivered frequently, I believe that it garnered the least resistance from the kids in terms of eye rolls and deep breaths, because I rarely droned on about rights and responsibilities. I wanted to burn this one into their brains through short and sweet repetition, because reasons to give this lecture presented themselves almost daily and the concept was very simple – with every right comes responsibility.

I repeated this concept year after year as the children earned more rights by simply getting older. They were not perfect in terms of accepting responsibility, but raising perfect children was never the goal. The goal was that they would hear the concept so many times that it would be ingrained in them when they left the comfortable nest. Below are a few examples.

- "With the right to live in the house comes the responsibility to keep your room clean and help with daily chores."

- "With the right to have a dog, comes the responsibility to help exercise, feed and clean up after the dog."

- "With the right to make independent decisions comes the responsibility to understand that those decisions have consequences."

- "With the right to drive a car comes the responsibility to use your head, follow the law and drive carefully so you don't hurt anyone."

- "With the right to date comes the responsibility to treat your date and his/her parents with respect."

- "With the right to vote comes the responsibility to get informed about the issues that impact this country."

- "With the right to buy alcohol at age 21 comes the responsibility to not be the conduit for your younger brother or sister to get alcohol."

- "With the right to be a parent comes the responsibility to raise the child."

In writing this book and speaking to my kids, I found out that my oldest son did in fact buy beer for his younger (and underage) brother and sister a few times. Brett actually had the nerve to defend this to me by using a parenting lecture saying, "Dad, I understand that you had to give me that lecture about not buying them beer in order to do the right thing as a parent. However, you did teach me about rights and responsibilities. You have to understand that with the right to be the older brother comes the responsibility to help out Matt and Kelsey once in a while. I promise that I gave them all the moderation lectures that you gave us and made the point that 'Dad will kill me if he finds out, so he better never find out'. And look, you never found out." Wow. I didn't even know how to respond to him.

Hmmm. I never found out. Put differently, he never got caught. When one of them did get caught, the third foundation lecture took a different turn towards arguably it's most important part – the consequences. The true tying together of rights and responsibilities came when the children lost specific rights because they didn't take responsibility to maintain those rights. These consequences, commonly known as "loss of privileges" or "grounding" and even "time out" and "spankings" when they were really young, were always framed around rights and responsibilities. I understood that the loss of rights was what made them want to take more responsibility to earn them back – and getting them to take more responsibility was the main objective.

There was always a bit of "God Bless America" behind the rights and responsibilities lectures. This was a carryover from my Dad who often framed the responsibility part of his lectures around the flag. Remember, Dad was part of the greatest generation (Army Signal Corps during WWII, stationed in New Guinea) and he was compelling to listen to when he got on country. He would point to two of the primary documents in American history and start a lecture about rights and responsibilities: "The Declaration of Independence states that we have inalienable rights endowed by our Creator; the U.S. Constitution and the first ten amendments defining the Bill of Rights assures us essential rights and liberties as U.S. citizens."

I would wonder, "What is this, history class?"

He would continue, "These documents are foundation builders in their own right and have established the principles and values upon which this great country was built. A strong foundation is just as important for the country as it is for the individual. You need to understand that your generation is the future. If we build strong foundations in our children, the likelihood that the foundation of the country will stay strong increases."

He wanted me to understand that the rights that I often took for granted just because I was born in America did not come without sacrifice. As a country, we needed to work hard to maintain the foundation upon which freedom was built. "You kids are the future and that is why I am pushing the basics so hard. If you build a solid individual foundation, it continues to strengthen the country that you and your children and their children will call home."

Finally, he would get to the hit your knees part which signaled closing, "When you hit your knees and count your blessings tonight, start with the fact that you were born in this country. Many have come before you and sacrificed their lives to make this country what it is today. By virtue of simply being born here, you have rights that many in the world can only hope for. With those rights comes the responsibility to participate in America, respect our history, and recognize that while the United States isn't perfect, it is the most generous, opportunity-laden country in the world. We have spilled more American blood helping others than any other country on this planet. People from all over the world are lining up to come to America — and have for many, many, decades. You need to recognize that with the right to be an American comes some serious responsibility." Like most members of the Greatest Generation, my Dad loved his country and passed that passion on to his kids often through the conduit of the third foundation lecture.

FOUNDATION LECTURE #4
SHOW UP

Based on the way my Dad often delivered this lecture, it could also have been called the "Quit bitching and show up" lecture. It rounds out the foundation lectures because it serves as a catch-all for the three that precede it. The faith, balanced life and rights/responsibilities lectures are all well and good, but they don't really matter much if you don't show up and live your life. The rationale behind this as a foundation point was that everything that was going on in a balanced life was important enough for the kids to show up and put their best effort forward.

While the way my Dad gave this lecture was in an aggressive posture – "Quit bitching and show up" – I gave it as more of a surrender cry - "Please show up." This happened because I found myself often ending arguments with my children as follows:

"We have had some good discussion about this, and you have made some good points. However, I am asking you to sacrifice and show up for me on this one. This is important to your Mother and me and we are asking you to come with a good attitude. And I mean a good attitude. I'd rather have you not come at all than have you pout and sulk the whole time."

Any of the children would tread cautiously here, still trying to get out of something they didn't particularly want to do, "Well, then maybe I shouldn't go."

"That is up to you. You are old enough to make this decision on your own. I am asking you to do this as a favor to your Dad. Show up for me please."

This was my exit line whenever I was able to stay calm enough in an argument with the kids to deliver it. I think that all three of my children actually bailed on me a couple of times each in a situation like this – but overall their percentage of showing up was more than commendable. After years of having to end thousands of debates with the kids this way, it became a foundation lecture in its own right. This was a good thing because the lecture actually became more meaningful as the kids entered their teen and early adult years and assumed more responsibilities. It provided a good transition into the real-world lectures – where you have to show up.

There was a non-defensive version of this lecture that was given to the kids from the time they started school until they left the nest. It was basic, motivational, and given often. If I was waiting on Kelsey to get ready so we could go somewhere, I would sit down in her room as she got dressed and say something like, "You know, life itself is not a dress rehearsal - you get one shot in your short time here to live your life the right way. Enjoy it, celebrate it, and for crying out loud, show up for it. At this point you are only 7, but you still need to show up everyday – and you are. You are showing up as a wonderful daughter for Mom and me and as a sister to both of your brothers. You are showing up as a student....as a friend...as a granddaughter...as a teammate. Showing up keeps you busy. You should look at every day this way: *I get to show up today!* Are you with

70

me?" She smiles at funny Daddy, nods and hugs me. This is a prime example of me overdoing the foundation lectures a bit. As Julie would say, "For goodness sakes Ted, she is seven!" I figured no harm, no foul and lectured on.

Most of the foundation lectures I gave transitioned well one into the other. For example, I could argue that showing up for any part of your balanced life triggered rights and responsibilities. That's three of the four sermons right there. The more they tied together, the more likely they were to stick. The long-term objective of the series was to build a solid foundation under the children through the repetition of the basics. The nearer term objective of the last speech was to get the kids to understand that they needed to show up, stay active, and live their life to the fullest everyday. I believed that if they tried to do that, they would be busy young people and avoid the frightening fact that "Idle hands are the devil's tools" as the vulnerable teenage years approached. I already had the next set of lectures ready to go.

HAPPY HOLIDAYS FROM THE HENDERSONS

Well another year has passed and I'm beginning to dread writing this letter. As I search for content, I'm struck by the obvious fact that we are boring people. We live in a "Stepfordesque" triangle between home, office, and schools and are only attempting to maintain the bare minimum basics --- AND MAN, ARE WE TIRED!! Julie and I both believe that the sacrifices we are making now will payoff in the future when the kids fill Mile High Stadium with 75,000 people to honor us as "The Best Parents in the World." In the meantime, I'm looking forward to meeting my wife again.

My own parents' response to my complaining comes with an arrogant assuredness that all of this sacrifice is ultimately worthwhile --- "Quit whining. We already put our time in. Bring us the grandchildren. This is what we have been waiting for." They stand as tangible proof that the holy grail of a loving, close knit, family is attainable through the boring maintenance of the basics – and it is in that realization that we are truly blessed.

Anyway, holiday letter tradition now requires that I update you on our lives. (Not that you're really that interested – it's tradition.) In our case, we have to own up to the fact that there isn't anything different about us since tradition last required that I update you 12 months ago. I work, coach and do what Julie tells me to do; Julie is Ubermom (currently trying to figure out a way to get a dining room table in the car – since most meals are eaten there anyway); the kids – (Brett 13 with a deep voice, Matthew 11 with an attitude, and Kelsey 8 with a cause) – enjoy/tolerate school, friends, church, well balanced meals, sports, activities, 'R' rated movies on cable when Julie and I are out on a date, and family. Not a Mozart, Einstein, or Picasso among them, but they are well balanced with a love of family, lots of friends and lots of activities. Oh yeah, Polly the Bulldog (banished from this year's picture for being 4 ½ years old and not yet housebroken) is still colossally dumb.

I could attempt a more elaborate prose, making things sound a little more exciting/better than they really are, but I think you'd see through it – and the cynic in me makes me frightened of what you'd see. I know that when I read in someone's Christmas letter that – "Tommy, our oldest, is 14 and showing entrepreneurial tendencies and a real head for business. He took time this summer to learn about the legislative, executive and judicial branches of our government – and still found time to spend a month at an exclusive summer camp! He met a new friend who is going to stay in close touch with him throughout the upcoming year," -- I read a little deeper and see the following: "Tommy was caught attempting to sell small packets of baby powder to an undercover policeman for $100 each. He was charged as a minor and sentenced to 1 month at a halfway house and 1-year probation." It is all in the way one interprets things.

I'd hate to think of how you might interpret something like this – "Julie and I have been married for 16 years and still manage to find life with each other fresh and exciting. We are inordinately proud of our kids and the lives they are building for themselves. Life is good." At least life is good at this point. We are now entering the teenage years and Julie and I are prepared to hold on for dear life as the children navigate this bridge to adulthood. Hopefully we won't have a "Tommy" situation where we have to re-write history in our upcoming annual letters. Brett is officially a teenager, Matthew about a year and a half away, and Kelsey will effectively be a teenager at age 11 because of her older brothers. We are scared of them. We are going to focus our next generation parenting efforts on getting the kids to avoid the "huge mistake". We have a plan – now the storm starts. We wish all of you a Merry Christmas and a healthy and happy New Year 1996!

Love, Ted, Julie, Brett, Matthew and Kelsey

CHAPTER 5
THE STAYING ALIVE LECTURES

The staying alive lectures were delivered throughout the teen years when the kids were exposed to more than any parent should ever have to deal with. The lectures were created because I realized that the stakes would rise for my kids in every way imaginable during these years and I needed to maintain and build on our established dialogue while they were going crazy. After drilling home the foundation lectures largely as a one-way oratory, the teenage years would bring more interaction and confrontation into the mix. I recognized it as simply the teenage way - I had, after all, been one too.

I needed to approach these lectures cautiously so I wouldn't lose standing with the kids. Credibility was a must when talking to the kids about the serious issues of drinking, drugs and sex. Of course, I was a wreck during these years, but I held onto an awkward comfort that I had somehow survived my own teenage years. That didn't stop the worry gene from kicking in after going briefly dormant in the shadow of the kids building a fairly strong foundation - I knew that I had entered the parenting stage where my control over things was diminishing rapidly.

I took my recollections of my own teenage experiences and projected them on to my kids, figuring they were running at a clip two years ahead of my pace from twenty years ago. It took me about a week to recover from this realization. I worried whenever the kids left the comfortable nest; not obsessively, just parentally. However, away from the home was the ultimate parenting goal, so I lectured my way through the teenage years by the seat of my pants, prayed, and held on for dear life.

STAYING ALIVE LECTURE # 1
KEEP IT BETWEEN THE FENCE POSTS

The staying alive lectures didn't start until I had already earned some credibility with the kids. Some of what I said in the foundation lectures apparently made sense, so listening to Dad talk was now something that the kids took for granted. With these sermons, I would simply ask them to sit down because I had something important to talk about. Having kids that are receptive to a common-sense message is just as important as the message itself and I was always thankful for the respectful audience that my children gave me.

I knew that I would lose them if I approached the topics in a strict, legalistic manner: "Sex is for marriage only," "You should never touch a drop of alcohol until you are 21," "Pot, like all drugs will kill you." While the legalistic abstinence route was an admirable goal that we supported and communicated, I felt that preaching these words alone and then washing my hands of the matter would be leaving my kids unarmed for what they would actually face in terms of majority peer pressure to experiment in these areas. Discipline and moderation seemed to be the rational companions to abstinence, so I developed the "Keep it Between the Fence Posts" lecture, which went something like this:

"Mom and I are very proud of the young man/woman you are becoming. You have built a solid foundation and are on track to lead a productive life. Thirteen years old is an important hurdle – you are now a teenager, no longer a child. I want to talk to you about what becoming a teenager means, so you understand how Mom and I are looking at things. This is going to be an important lecture, so I want your attention. Okay?" I got an imperceptible nod.

I continued, "First, becoming a teenager means that you are now officially starting on the path to adulthood. You will acquire a lot more rights over the next few years and you need to understand your responsibilities. I want to use a visual, like the balanced life hand lecture, to get you to burn out a neuron on this one. Okay? I want you to picture a long bridge, like the Golden Gate Bridge. You know what that looks like, right?" Yes, from one of the worst Bond movies ever, *A View to a Kill*.

"That bridge represents the teenage years - a linking of childhood and adulthood. Basically, we want you to reach adulthood without driving off the bridge. This lecture isn't going to address specific stuff like drinking, drugs, and sex even though those are the types of things you are going to encounter as you cross the bridge. This lecture is more about the big picture. We want you to navigate the bridge with discipline and maturity. While you are crossing the bridge, we want you to keep your behavior between the big orange fence posts - don't drive off the bridge. Understand what I am saying? We want you to make good decisions and avoid the huge mistake." I got a nod and continued.

"Now, imagine a white line running down the middle of the bridge. That line is the straight and narrow. The objective is to stay close to the straight and narrow line. I know that can be difficult and I believe that most kids probably step off the line and experiment with say, drinking in high school. I am not approving of that. It is against the law and if you choose to drink while underage and get caught, you will suffer legal as well as parental consequences. However, I want you to understand that if you are using moderation and discipline, tiptoeing off the straight and narrow once in a while is normal and unlikely to get you into huge trouble."

"On the other hand, if we see you going off the bridge, if you can't show discipline and keep your behavior between the fence posts, then we are going to intervene aggressively. If you are making such poor decisions that you are careening all over the bridge and your life is in jeopardy, then we are going to step in. You will lose all rights as you know them, and we will go back to the drawing board to figure out where we went wrong in messaging to you. Do you understand me?" Solemn nod.

"Good. You know that life is precious, a gift from God. You also need to understand that life is fragile. Teenagers believe they are bulletproof and that nothing can hurt them. You are not bulletproof. We are talking about this now, because I believe that you are going to encounter some of these things in the near future, if you haven't already. All those specific discussions will be with the 'Keep it between the fence posts' concept in the background. Okay?" I got a final nod. "We love you and want you to make it safely to adulthood."

The challenge of this homily was the Catch-22 of acknowledging likely teenage behavior that was off the straight and narrow, and "green lighting" such behavior because of the acknowledgement. It was difficult (and no fun) to pilot this line but, like all parents, we tried our best and then hoped and prayed.

STAYING ALIVE LECTURE # 2
DRINKING

The ultimate Catch 22 category was underage drinking. How does a parent acknowledge underage drinking as a likely occurrence without green lighting a child to experiment and indulge? Again, I had also been a teenager and had managed keep enough brain cells alive so that I had a good idea of what I was up against. Most of my personal memories about underage drinking end with my head in the toilet, getting violently sick. This predictable ending had nothing to do with how much I drank, just that I drank at all. Alcohol and I just have never really agreed with each other. Julie doesn't drink much either, so we have one of the worst stocked liquor cabinets around, as any of our friends who drop by unannounced can attest. "Umm, let's see here. Can we offer you some water?"

I knew that the fact that we didn't drink much and had little alcohol around the house would have absolutely no impact on our own children and the decisions they would make regarding alcohol. My view of teenage consumption was that it was a simple matter of statistics: Most teenagers would try alcohol while underage. Some, after trying, would just not be that interested in alcohol for a number of reasons, like me. Some would imbibe with moderation and discipline and rarely get out of control. Interestingly this often seemed to be the guy who had managed to get the fake ID — he was somewhat in control because he apparently felt the need to take some responsibility for providing the alcohol and he was probably also the driver.

Others would always overindulge and be constantly out of control — "Come on pussy! Punch me in the face! I can take it. Hit me as hard as you can right in the face."

I would always reply, "I don't want to hit you. You are one of my best friends. Why would I hit you?"

He would slur, "To prove you're a not a woman. Now hit me right here on the chin, I can take it." Most people knew a guy like this in high school and, not to stereotype, but he was almost always a football player.

Finally, some kids would indulge while underage and unfortunately lose the battle with alcohol and have it sadly define their life. As a parent, I had no idea which category my children would fall in to, which made the topic scary and uncomfortable like all parenting topics that address the unknown. Further, once the kids became mobile there was no real control any longer, they were essentially independent and making their own decisions. This lack of control was a change from the feeling I had while trying to help develop their foundation.

I took comfort in the fact that teenagers today are much more aware of the serious consequences that accompany underage drinking, and especially underage drinking and driving, than we were in my day. I remember driving some high school friend's home in 1974 (I was 17 at the time) and being pulled over for rolling through a stop sign at a little past midnight. Everyone in the car was still in high school, we were out past curfew, we had open beer in the car, and none of us would have passed a sobriety test. We were only about a mile from home and the (very nice) police man poured out all of our beer, told us to stay out of trouble and to get home safely. That was it.

Comparing that experience to the way high school kids who get caught with beer today are treated tells a significant story about the way things have changed, and the awareness level of the issue among the young. Minor in Possession (MIP) tickets and community service are commonplace today as the minimum punishment a young man or woman making this decision and getting caught faces. A lot of good kids try alcohol while underage and when they get caught the first time, their life should not end. The MIP ticket and community service seem to send the right message for first time offenders, and because of this it seems that all teenagers are aware of the serious consequences for these actions. That awareness level did not exist when I was a teenager, so progress has been made.

That said there are certain protected species that are apparently still not aware of the consequences of underage drinking today. For example, the young, Hollywood elite appear to be somewhat clueless about this fact, along with millions of other things. I mean how often do we see pictures of underage starlets out partying in night clubs while underage? Any consequences? Nope. Not until they hit someone with their car or get caught driving the wrong way on a one-way street while hammered, like recent parenting award winner Nicole Ritchie before she became a mother, but after she had kicked her heroin habit.

I always felt that *"Us Magazine"* should be called *"Them Magazine"*, because I'm sorry but I just can't relate. I love that Bernie Goldberg began his book, "The 100 People Who Are Screwing Up America", with Rick and Kathy Hilton (Paris Hilton's parents) at the top of the list. His inclusion of them in the number one position underscores what I think is a widely held belief that involved parents with common sense matter – and those that choose to not be involved with their kids, and don't apply common sense in raising them, are kind of screwing up America.

Sorry - end of unpaid political commentary. Back to teenage drinking. I refused to be naïve on the subject of drinking when it came to my own kids. I was going to assume they would probably experiment with alcohol in high school. Weirdly, I was okay with this. Right or wrong, I didn't want them getting to college with absolutely no partying experience and then going crazy, because that too was a recipe for disaster. I was going to be open and talk to my kids about this in a forthright manner, preaching abstinence, moderation, discipline, and good judgment when it came to drinking. There was an absolute zero tolerance for drinking and driving, and we had all agreed that Dad would come anywhere, anytime to get one of them if they called – with no consequences.

I told the kids what I truly believed - that a little bit of alcohol or a little bit of pot was not going to kill anyone. This was, however, only true if employing discipline and moderation. Any other drugs should be viewed as a death sentence. I thought that this approach was sensible and would keep my credibility in place with the kids. In being honest about my own experiences, when they asked, I told them that while I hardly drank at all in college, I did do some inhaling.

College hoops in the '70s, you know. Hanging out and listening to Richard Pryor, the Commodores, Ohio Players, Brick, and Brothers Johnson, talking trash and playing card games on road trips in all the SEC cities. Yeah, I hung out with some ball players and smoked some pot in college – and I told my kids about it. In admitting this I added that I was always on top of my grades and my other responsibilities first. I partied, but I always made sure I had earned the right to party. (Okay, have I justified the fact that I smoked pot enough yet? I hated admitting this to my kids.) This "earning the right to party" notion was conceptually was a throwback to the connecting of work and play in the balanced life lecture.

Whenever I talked about drinking or pot, I always made an implied closing point, which probably made me a bad Dad. I told them, "Don't get caught." I made this point in a very simple and straightforward manner because the concept was easy to communicate, "Underage drinking and pot are illegal. Period. You have to follow the law and if you get caught breaking the law there are consequences. So first make the decision to stay away from both completely, and if you can't do that then do not get caught!"

I lectured on, "Most kids are doing the same basic stuff – and have been for decades and decades. Your Grandmother drank alcohol while in high school, and that was in the 1940s, so this is not new stuff. If you are using your head and employing discipline, the likelihood that you will get caught just off the straight and narrow is small. However, if you are out of control with alcohol and drugs the likelihood that you drive off the bridge is, no pun intended, high."

I continued, "If you do get caught, that changes the landscape because you move into what we call the no tolerance zone. That means you have already screwed up once, so you can't afford to screw up again. That means that 'Don't get caught' just went out the door. It is replaced by 'You must completely abstain to get back into good graces.'" Thankfully I had an arsenal of examples that I could point to about people who get caught and then keep screwing up.

Mike Tyson always led off this list as payback for the sex discussion I had with Matthew because of him.

STAYING ALIVE LECTURE # 3
THE SEX STUFF

The sex stuff hangs in the background and is not really an issue until parents must confront the inevitable first step - explaining to the kids where babies come from. For my parent's generation, the birds and bees discussion was generally the beginning and the end of sex conversation with their children. For us, the MTV generation of parents, we have to talk about sex beyond the birds and bees basics with our charges because sex, especially with the advent of the Internet, is now everywhere. Since my Dad was an overachiever, he made sure that I got two discussions about the fact of life basics.

The first one I only remember vaguely, as I was a bit too young. It was a summer weekend, and Dad had called me in from playing outside saying, "Hey, Ted. Come on in here and sit down with your Dad. I want you to listen to something with me." Dad apparently just felt it was the right time for me to hear about the facts of life - I certainly hadn't asked any questions yet.

I came inside and sat down as Dad retrieved a record album. He pulled out the vinyl disc, handed me the cover and put the record on. I was just getting into music, so I looked with interest at the album cover which wasn't very interesting compared to a Beatles or Rolling Stones cover. The cover was a picture of a young boy who was feeding a horse a carrot. I was wondering what this was all about when Dad said, "I want you to listen to this with me and then we can talk about it afterwards, okay?"

I was looking at the album cover thinking about how cool it would be to have a horse that I could feed carrots to and absently said, "Sure."

My Dad started the record while I stared at the album cover wondering why there wasn't any music playing. To my disappointment, the record was nothing but a guy taking to his son about something that I couldn't follow. What I heard made no sense to me and seemed to have nothing to do with a horse or a carrot. By the time the guy said, "The baby then grows in the Mommy's stomach" I was completely lost. What baby? What stomach? What about the kid feeding the horse the carrot? I assumed that was important to the story, I mean it made the album cover.

The record ended, and my Dad asked me, "Do you understand what we just listened to?"

I lied, "I think so." Then I gestured to the album cover and asked, "What does the boy feeding the horse the carrot have to do with anything?"

My Dad answered, "Nothing at all. It is just a picture of a young boy about your age who is curious."

"Curious about what?"

"Well, curious about what the Dad and the son were talking about. You know, how babies come into the world."

I pointed to the boy, "Is the boy the son?"

My Dad said, "Probably."

"Why didn't the Dad talk about him about his horse? Do all horses like carrots?"

My Dad shook his head, "Because the horse and the carrot have nothing to do with anything. The boy is just curious about where babies come from."

"Where is the baby?" Gesturing with the album cover, "Why isn't there a baby picture on here? Why is the horse even eating a carrot?"

It was at this point that my Dad came to the conclusion that I was too young – or too gay, given my obsession with the boy, the horse and the carrot – for the birds and the bees discussion. I remember him kind of abruptly ending this father/son bonding session and sending me out to play.

The second facts of life conversation came about a year later. My brother and I were walking to the store one evening and were about two blocks away from the house when I asked him a question about something I had heard. He stopped and said, "We have to go back home."

"Why?" I asked.

He didn't say another word until we walked into the house where he yelled, "Mom, Dad, come down here please." When Mom and Dad came downstairs, my brother simply pointed at me and said, "He asked" and left the room. I was furious with him. I remember thinking I might be in trouble given my questions – the Catholic guilt was very present at this point in my life.

My Mom and Dad sat me down and told me that I was asking perfectly normal questions and then proceeded to tell me all about the birds and the bees in their wonderful, loving parental manner – without a record guiding them. I was glad they both were there because Dad seemed on the brink on this subject and he got out of sync early in our discussion when I asked if this had anything to do with the boy, the horse, and the carrot.

He lost his cool and said, "For crying out loud Ted. Will you please just forget about the boy the horse and the carrot? Lord! That has absolutely nothing to do with what we are talking about here. It was just a picture of a curious boy, nothing more. I don't know why the horse was there eating a carrot. I am sorry I tried that record. Biggest mistake I could have made. Now, let it go! Please!" My Mom got him back on track and they performed admirably, together teaching me the facts of life.

So, I got all my questions answered that night, including the mortifying "So do you and Mom still…you know…even though you have already had us three kids?"

Dad answered this, not Mom, and said, "I want you to understand that a man and a woman who are married and in love don't only make love to each other to have babies. Making love is a physical expression of affection for each other – like kissing, only much closer, more intimate. It is a very important, ongoing part of a relationship when a man and a woman are in love and married. So, the answer is yes."

I still haven't recovered from that one, although I often repeat the line to Julie about sex being "a very important, ongoing part of a relationship when a man and a woman are in love and married." She ignores me.

For my children, there were myriad lectures that touched on sex beyond the birds and bees basics. The marketing of sex was beginning to explode when I was a kid in the 60's and 70's and it had become a full-blown smorgasbord of availability with the Internet and cable television by the time my kids became teenagers. I believed that lovingly explaining the birds and the bees to the kids wasn't going to be enough to ensure a healthy attitude towards sex for them given outside influences. I definitely wanted them to have a healthy, non-guilty view of sex given my own experiences.

As a Catholic teenager I was so guilt ridden about anything having to do with sex that I went to confession and confessed to masturbation as a sin. It wasn't that anyone had addressed masturbation with me or indicated that it was a sin. I was a Catholic - anything that felt that good and had to do with that part of your body was a sin in my young mind.

When I could carry my escalating guilt no further, I finally broke down and admitted to the sin of masturbation in confession, "Bless me Father for I have sinned. It has been one week since my last Confession. My sins are...umm...I have been swearing sometimes, but not the Lord's name. I have been mean to my sister and have told some lies to my parents. I lost my temper when playing sports and got into a fight. I tried to get my brother in trouble for something that I broke the other day. Ummm....I have....ummm....kind of been touching myself .....kind of....ummmm...in my private parts area until I can't take it any more. I know this is a sin. So, for these sins I have now said and for those sins I have forgotten, I am heartily sorry."

The kindly Priest started by addressing my last confessed sin. "My son, I want you to know that it is normal for a young man to touch himself in the manner you described - and it is definitely not a sin."

Now, at the time, I didn't recognize him as the expert on the subject that I am now certain he was. I did recognize him as a Catholic Priest who had a direct link to God, and he had just told me that what I had been doing and feeling guilty about was not a sin. He might as well have said, "My son, why does a dog lick his balls?" to me.

I am sure that he addressed my other sins, gave me penance and absolution - but I can't swear to it. I didn't hear another word he said after, "definitely not a sin." From that moment on I could think of nothing else but the countless ways I was going to pleasure myself when I got home. I don't think I came out of my room for four days. No meals, no nothing.

I was going to do everything I could to make sure that my kids had a healthy view of sex, sans guilt. So, I insisted that the kids come to me with any questions about sex, and I would do my best to answer them truthfully. Even if they didn't specifically ask me, I found easy ways to bring the topic of sex into the conversation if I wanted to trigger a lecture. I understood that to address a topic like pornography all I had to do was show up and be remotely aware. Again, I thought about what I would have been doing at that age, and Internet porn, had it existed, would have stood near the top of my "Must have some" list at age 14.

Based on the Delta Force type missions I went on with buddies back in the 1970s to secure a soiled Playboy magazine from a trash can just to see some naked breasts, I think I can confidently say I would have found an Internet connection and seen some porn. So, I understood my adversary's mindset, which is always helpful. Not to discriminate, but in our house, porn was strictly a boy issue. Kelsey was into IM and chat and that was frightening enough, but no porn for her, at least not at our house.

We tried to make access to the Internet and premium cable channels as difficult as possible in our home. There was a computer on the main floor, and the kids were not allowed televisions or computers in their bedrooms. This, I knew, was not necessarily the case at all their friend's homes. I already assumed they were seeing porn outside of the comfortable nest and there was not much that I could do about that. It was my job to make access to inappropriate material in the home as difficult as possible – and to explain what they might be seeing outside of the home to them. A common theme in our parenting was to try to make it as hard as possible for the kids to get into trouble, while still addressing the issues head on. So, I talked to them:

"I want to talk to you guys about pornography. Pornography is a form of entertainment for adults that is designed, like all entertainment, to elicit a certain response from the audience. This type of entertainment is no different from a horror movie that is designed to scare the audience, a comedy that is designed to make the audience laugh, or an adventure movie that is designed to get our toes tingling. Porn movies and Internet porn are designed to get a response from you know where - and they work. However, none of them are real!"

"We have talked about this many times and you guys know that there is nothing more special than an intimate relationship between a man and a woman who are in love and trust each other. That is what sex is all about – intimate relationships that are based on more than just the physical act. Porn is only about the physical act. Mom and I trust that you will make good decisions about the pace at which your sexual experiences progress and this porn stuff doesn't help if you think it represents real life in any way. These are not real people. These are actors trying to make a buck so they can pay their bills. There is a market for the stuff they are selling. But it is not real!"

"No nurse is ever going to suddenly start having sex with you when you visit the doctor for a physical. No stewardess is ever going to want to meet you in the lavatory and have sex with you on a flight. No cheerleader is ever going to take you to the 50-yard line for sex. No lonely housewife is going to invite you in for sex and lemonade after mowing her lawn. A female cable installer will not have sex with you in front of the television. It only happens in porn movies." Okay, so I've seen some porn in my lifetime. I figured I had covered 95% of porn movie plots with the nurse, stewardess, lonely housewife, and cheerleader characters. The cable installer was a personal nod to my own career.

I continued, "You need to be aware that porn is usually degrading to women and that real women are not like what you see in porn movies. They do not respond to the way men act in porn movies in the real world. Women need to be treated with love, respect, affection and thoughtfulness. That is not what you generally see in porn movies. That is because porn movies are not real!"

"That said I want you to know that I understand your interest in adult stuff like this because I was interested at your age also. I am painfully aware of the fact that you have probably seen much worse than I saw at your age already. While it is normal to be curious, this porn stuff can be addicting. It falls into the staying alive lecture where I want you to keep your adult access 'Between the fence posts'. I want you to respect your Mom and sister. That means I don't want any of this stuff in our home, understand me?"

Other topics surrounding sex were just as easy to infiltrate as porn was. Again, all I had to do was be remotely aware and available to talk to my kids. I had my agenda for them, and I lectured frequently about the fact that sex has consequences and tied this to the foundation lecture on rights and responsibilities. We made it clear that a sexual awakening was completely normal in teenagers and that sexual exploration should only be done with someone you trust, respect, and love. We acknowledged that the pace at which teenagers explore can vary greatly and we encouraged a moderate pace. "Don't be in such a hurry" seemed like good advice sexually from many vantage points.

While we said that intercourse was for marriage only, our kids were living in the late 1990s and early 2000s and were aware that this was not the case among many of the people that they knew. In addition to the high profile that AIDS and STDs had in the kids' minds, pregnancy was also an obvious consequence of sexual activity. We preached that no one should be having sex if they weren't ready to become a parent. While the consequence of pregnancy wasn't a death sentence like AIDS, becoming a teenage parent would without question be life altering and cause the kids to miss out on the wonderful young adult years as they took on the responsibility of raising a child. This approach was the best way we knew to maintain credibility with our kids and still send an abstinence message on the sex front. It was a fine line to navigate – and no fun as a parent.

The three staying alive lectures stood alone, with no direct ties to the foundation or real-world lectures. However, the three are more connected as a series than either of the others. The staying alive lectures were all about disciplined performance and personal responsibility within a balanced life. They were about how to tilt the scales in your favor with good decision making to allow you to safely reach adulthood and all its great mysteries of independence. They were about not being in such a hurry to grow up, "Life is not a sprint; it is a long race - pace yourself in the journey to adulthood."

In safely navigating the bridge they arrived at the real-world lectures and brought me not a moment's rest. Certainly, there should be something for a parent beyond a college tuition bill that awaits a survivor of the high school years.

HAPPY HOLIDAYS FROM THE HENDERSONS

As in prior years, I have delivered many drafts of this year's holiday letter to Julie for her review and sign off. Each and every one (so far) has been dismissed with extreme prejudice. I apparently have struggled to find an appropriate holiday tone. The events of September 11th certainly can't go unmentioned in a correspondence to our friends and family members at this time of year. While all Americans have been profoundly affected, we especially want to send our thoughts to those of you that were directly and personally impacted by the tragedy.

The problem with most of the previous letter drafts was that I apparently included some indiscriminate Arab bashing in virtually every letter. Julie found this politically incorrect, and in many cases downright offensive. She would have no part of it in our Christmas letter and sent me back to try again...and again. As usual, the democratic process prevailed at the Henderson home: Democrat Julie got her way over Republican Ted. Accordingly, I will hold back my incisive political commentary and resort to a standard update on the family.

Ted is in job transition and Julie is carrying the work load at Pre-school this year. She really loves being with the kids and enjoys the people she works with. My schedule has consisted of driving the car pool, running any and all errands, working out, going to matinee movies, playing golf and finding new TV shows to watch. I don't really understand how my schedule (or lack thereof) affects Julie, but the message is clear: I need to find a job soon or the marriage is in jeopardy. I think the tipping point for Julie was my recent suggestion that we spend more time together.

Brett (19) is a sophomore at Colorado State and is enjoying college life immensely. He was home for Thanksgiving and Julie and I marveled at the calming presence he had on Matthew and

Kelsey's relationship. We miss him greatly for this reason alone. I forgot to tell you in last years letter - Brett voted (as a Republican) in his first Presidential election last year. He claimed Republican status when he was filling out his voter registration form and turned to Julie to ask, "Who hates everybody, Republicans or Democrats?"

Julie, of course, didn't hesitate and answered, "Republicans."

I was about to argue this when Brett went, "I guess I'm a Republican." I am so proud.

Matthew (17) is a senior in high school and is still undecided as to where he will attend college next year. We hope that being away at college will help Matthew to appreciate our parenting efforts so that he will show us a little more respect. Until then his template response to any of my attempts at father/son conversation is some variation of, "You know what Dad? You are a fat, balding old guy with slowly developing man breasts. Please stay away from me." It seems to strike Matthew as hysterical when he says this, but I don't see the humor. Plus, I take major issue with one of his assertions. My man breasts are actually developing quite fast, just like another Lefty - Phil Mickelson.

Kelsey (14) is in 8th grade and is one year away from being an only child of sorts. She is very excited about the prospect of not sharing Mom and Dad with the boys. Julie and I are nervous, as we don't think we can handle Kelsey all by ourselves. Kelsey is a teenage girl who knows all the right buttons to push to drive her Dad crazy -- excessive phone time, excessive on-line time, and dating Arabs.

WE SINCERELY HOPE YOU HAVE A WONDERFUL HOLIDAY SEASON
AND A HAPPIER 2002
Love, Ted, Julie, Brett, Matthew and Kelsey

CHAPTER 6
THE REAL WORLD LECTURES

Like their staying alive predecessors, the real-world lectures were delivered over a relatively short timeframe when compared to the long-term attempts at foundation building. However, these lectures had a longer shelf life. They were designed to get the kids to think like adults so they could survive and flourish in a competitive world. They were also structured to ensure that the kids would eventually move out of the house and start paying for things themselves. I believe that if we did everything right as parents and failed to drive home the real-world points, the kids would love their Dad and Mom (which is good) and never understand the need to leave the comfortable nest (which is bad).

The first two lectures are related because they are inescapably tied together: an education leads to a decent job; a decent job delivers an income; and an income facilitates a lifestyle. The third lecture on country was introduced earlier than the other two lectures as a throwback to my Dad's inclusion of God Bless America themes in his lectures on rights and responsibility.

These lectures encouraged more feedback and dialogue than ever before because the kids were now capable of arriving at conclusions that might be different from what I was presenting. They were beginning to challenge me more frequently which, I knew, was a good thing. It was indicative of independent minds that were about to get out on their own in the real world.

REAL WORLD LECTURE # 1
EDUCATION AND WORK

The education/work lecture has direct ties to two foundation lectures, living a balanced life and showing up. Work would substitute for education in the balanced life when the kids finished college, and I linked the two from day one. There can be little argument about the importance of education in today's world, how a good education absolutely shifts the landscape in the child's favor in their effort to lead independent and productive lives. Accordingly, we raised the kids to view college as an absolute given. We talked early and often about education in the comfortable nest and this push accelerated in high school where grades really started to matter for the first time. I sat down with each child and gave some version of the following lecture on the eve of their first day in high school.

"Your Mom and I are very excited for you as you start high school. We love you very much and are proud of you. You are generally making good decisions, leading a balanced life, taking responsibility, and showing up for life every day with a good attitude. You are very well prepared to embark on this next exciting chapter in your life. You will do great in high school if you show up and put your best effort forward."

"There are a few things I want to point out about high school that you need to know from an academic perspective. In high school the stakes rise, and not just in the area of staying alive, which we have already started to talk about. Academically things become a lot more serious in high school because your grades really start to matter for the first time and will determine where you can go to college. You will have to earn your way into college by establishing a good high school track record."

"There are a lot of distractions in high school, and you need to establish good study habits and be organized and diligent about getting all of your work done before you play. I just want you to understand that no matter how fun and exciting high school gets, you are still there to do a job – make grades so you can get to college. So, every day you need to stay on top of your game and compete academically in the classroom so that you can get into a college. This is all about work; it is just packaged right now as education. Like it or not, most of your life will be spent working. You need to get a college education so you can use your brain instead of your back to make a living. The brain will work a lot longer than the back will. So, go knock 'em dead at high school tomorrow and get off to a good start towards college."

I walked a fine line here, not wanting to send a message that the fun part of their life would end immediately after college and they should prepare to be workforce slaves for the next 40 years of their life. I didn't want to specifically send that message because they would realize it soon enough on their own. Work is work. I was honest about things, admitting that I wasn't in love with my job – it was work. "Work isn't supposed to be fun, although some people are lucky enough to do something they absolutely love and have fun in their jobs. I think that most people unfortunately, do not love their jobs. However, I take pride in doing my job well and in getting up everyday to support this family. I am proud of the company I work for, proud to be a part of the broad American workforce, proud to pay my taxes, and happy to enjoy the fruits of my labor. It is what you do as the head of a family. None of the things that we sometimes take for granted happen if I don't have a good job."

Sometimes, when I couldn't hide that I was a bit exhausted by work, one of my kids would try to comfort me. Predictably, I would miss this nurturing attempt and clumsily continue to be Dad, the annoying lecture guy. Such was the case one night when I was relaxing and watching a ballgame on TV with 17-year-old Brett. He casually asked me, "Dad, do you ever just get tired of the grind? You know, getting up and going to the same place to work every day? Doing the same thing almost every day? I mean do you ever just want to quit?" (Seven years later the answer would be a resounding "YES, to write a book", but for right now I was still raising kids.)

My ears perked up because I was concerned that his question was more about him than about me. I answered, "Absolutely I get tired of the grind, as does everybody. Work is often a grind, but you have to hang in there. The grind is defined as having somewhere to go and something to do each and every day, generally your job - or for you right now, school. You show up. Both work and school allow you to pass time productively and position you to do other things in your life that you truly enjoy. Remember how work connects with play? I deal with the grind like everyone else, it earns my play time."

I had answered his question reasonably and he seemed fine. I then went off on a lengthy tangent that was designed to make sure that this wasn't about him. Eventually he cut me off. "Dad stop it! Oh my gosh! I was just asking about you because you have seemed a little tired lately." He continued with a smile, "I didn't need the teen suicide lecture from you here. I mean, I am fine and not about to do something crazy. Okay? My life is good and I am happy. I was asking about you, for crying out loud. You need to relax. I'm worried about you." I was too, and not for the first time.

The fact is that I was starting to fray a bit around the edges – and this was seven years ago. I couldn't share with the children that this is what years and years of work and responsibility do to a guy – he loses it eventually. Given my discussion with Brett, it was probably pretty clear to him that I was starting to unravel. It was about this time that I first put the thought in the back of my mind that when the kids were all out of the house, I would seek a life change. Until then, I soldiered through, and my lectures about work were as much to convince me to hang in there as they were for the kids.

REAL WORLD LECTURE # 2
MONEY AND FINANCES

I was always very open with the kids about our finances and I shared with them how much we made, how much we spent, and how much we saved each month. This openness was a hangover from the way my Dad always talked to me about financial stuff when I was a kid. In my mind, it was important for the kids to understand our household finances, so they would have a sense of what it took to support themselves and/or a family when they left for the real world. Dad had managed to teach me some financial discipline, and I was a moron. So, I had hope for my kids if I started this early enough.

When I was a kid Dad used to take me to the bank with him and, because he was Dad, this meant that I was going to hear everything that he knew about what banks do. I would hold the paycheck and company deposits in my lap while he drove to the bank. I would watch him deposit his check and see him get some cash back. Sometimes we would visit the safe deposit box and Dad would point out the vault nearby where the real money was kept. On the drive home, I would look at his bank book and see where the deposit had been added as well as his balance.

I understood where the check came from and what it represented because on the way to the bank, my Dad would tell me it was as good as real money. "You see, every two weeks, I get a check from the company for the work I have done. That is why I get up every

94

morning, to go to work so I can earn this paycheck which is as good as cash. I put it in the bank so that the money is safe for our family. It pays for everything that we do. It buys food, clothes, heats the house, - all that stuff. None of that happens if I don't have a job where I can get up, go to work, get this check, and deposit it in the bank. You understand?"

Truth be told, no. But I didn't say so. It was the first time I had heard a financial lecture and I was more interested in the dead bug that was stuck on our windshield. This would not be the last time I got a financial lecture about banks, paychecks, checking accounts, savings accounts, interest rates, etc. from Dad, and eventually most of it stuck by the time I got to high school. Frankly, I thought this was overkill on his part and, in hindsight, I believe I was too young for many of Dad's financial lectures. Accordingly, I hadn't intended on giving financial lectures to my kids until they were in high school and dealing with summer jobs, their own cars, and their own budgets.

That view changed when the five of us were driving in downtown Denver one day and we passed through a section of town where many homeless people were wandering the streets. I took the opportunity to lecture the kids. "I want you to take a good look at these people. They are homeless and can't afford a place to live. They live here on the streets. I promise this will not happen to you if you get educated and show up for your life every day. If you establish a good foundation and stay away from any life-altering decisions, the financial side will follow, and you will never be homeless. I'm sorry, but I don't think many of these people have worked hard to build a strong foundation, took their education seriously, or managed to avoid bad decisions."

I looked at Julie, knowing she is poised as a Democrat to tell me what an insensitive jerk I am being. "Mom may feel that this is a bit harsh, and it might be. I don't want to be mean. I feel sorry for these people, and there are probably a lot of individual stories that would submarine my generalization about their lack of effort, but that's how I feel. I want you to know that there are ways to avoid this end result and it starts early in your life. If you make a real effort, things will turn out okay. I promise."

Brett asked, "Why don't they have jobs, Dad?"

"There are probably a lot of different reasons why not. Some have had some bad luck and are trying to get back on their feet and are trying to get work. Some are mentally disabled and wouldn't be capable of holding down a job even if they could get one. Others have stopped showing up completely and are happy to let the state and Federal government care for them - with our tax dollars." While this was over their heads and would be until they got their first real paycheck and wondered where all their money went, I always threw it in, so they would know early that our taxes paid for a lot of stuff.

I continued, "One thing I will bet that most of them have in common is no college degree. I can't tell you enough about how important getting a good education is. It leads to a good job."

Matthew responded, "Dad, you tell us how important that is like a hundred times a day."

"Good, you need to hear it that often, so it sticks."

At this point Kelsey, then 9, piped up. "Daddy?"

"Yes sweetheart."

"Why don't they have money?"

I answered, "Because they can't get a good job and keep it."

She pressed, "But why don't they get some money?"

I tried again, "Because without a good job, there is no money."

She also tried again, "I don't understand why they don't just go and get some money."

We went back and forth for a minute or so like this, with me repeatedly explaining that the lack of money was a direct result of the lack of a job. Frustrated, she finally asked her real question, "Daddy, why don't they just go to the wall and get some money?"

Finally, it dawned on me. My 9-year-old daughter had never seen the inside of a bank or seen me deposit a paycheck. She was a child of the electronic deposit. As far as she knew, money came from a wall – the ATM machines. When I needed money, I put a card into a wall and out came some money. I wanted to say, "You are right honey. If they are too stupid to figure out how to get the money out of the wall, they deserve to be homeless."

Instead, I took my daughter to the bank the next week and we had our first financial discussion. I told her about where Daddy goes every day and how he gets paid. I told her that the money coming from the ATM was my own money that I had already put into the wall (the bank). The punch line is that it's never too young to impart financial wisdom to your children. Kelsey believed that money came from a wall for the first 9 years of her life and she has spent like it truly does ever since.

I mentioned that I was open about money and finances throughout the children's lives and they had a sense of what it cost us to live the way we did. Their understanding of our monthly budget was a direct result of a repeatedly ignored request from me that spawned a financial lecture. The ignored request was, "Can you please turn off the lights when you leave a room?" The lecture that resulted became known as "Bill Night" and it started this way.

After again not having the lights turned off as I requested, I queried Matthew, "How much do you think it costs to have the lights on in our house every month?" I paused, as the seed of the Bill Night lecture formed. "In fact, get your brother and sister up here right now and sit down at the kitchen table. I am going to get my checkbook."

Matthew stomped off and screamed downstairs to his brother and sister, and then moaned, "Dad, not another lecture."

"Oh yes, another lecture, and this is an important one that I just made up because you guys never turn out the lights. Get them up here now!" The other kids showed up and we all sat down at the breakfast table. "We are going to talk about how much it costs to run this family – to feed us, clothe us, house us, transport us – what it costs to live."

I proceeded, "You kids will eventually be out on your own working and earning a paycheck. You need to understand what the essentials are to live and how far your paycheck will go. We have a lot of extras in our lives, things that are not necessary to live happily, but they are fun, and we can afford them because Dad has been lucky to have a decent paying job. We are not rich, I can promise you that. In fact, let's talk about rich for a moment."

I got some eye rolls. They were realizing that this was not a formed lecture, and that I could go anywhere for any length of time. "We are not rich. Get that into your heads. We are not rich. Rich means you don't have to work and you can still pay all your bills every month. If I lose my job, we will have to cut way back on what we spend – rich people don't do that. So, I am on top of every dime that we spend, and that is why we are sitting here tonight."

I pulled out my checkbook and started to go through some monthly bills, asking the kids what they thought it cost per month for each item. There were many items and I distinguished the necessities from the extras: mortgage payment, electric bill, water bill, car payments, car insurance, gasoline, telephone, clothes, dinner out, groceries, cable television, internet connection, cell phones, country club, health club, home owner's dues, car license fees and finally savings. And all this was AFTER Social Security, Medicare, Federal/State Income, and Federal/State Unemployment Taxes! It took us a long time to go through all this and I was aware that while they were tired of this, I was hitting home. They had no idea how much everything they took for granted cost every month. Hopefully they were thinking, "Dad is an animal as a provider!"

I took the opportunity here to make the point that they were spoiled. I quickly pointed out that I was also spoiled as a kid. I further pointed out that by any global standard, most American kids were spoiled and that we were lucky to live in America. "Mom and I want to spoil you and provide nice things for you. But I want you to know that all of it stops the moment you start to act spoiled and have an expectation, an entitlement attitude, that we owe you these things.

You have the right to be spoiled by us, because you are our children and we love you. You have the responsibility to not act like a spoiled brat and to understand that Dad works hard to provide all this stuff. It doesn't fall off trees, or just come out of a wall."

"Your Mom and I are going to do everything in our power to pay for your college, so you can graduate without owing anybody any money. That can give you a big head start in life, since quite a few people graduate from college and have to pay off student loans. So, if we are lucky enough to be in a position to pay for your college, we will, since you are living your life in a disciplined manner and appear to be on the right track to become a contributing member of society. College is a big part of your ability to do that, and we want to pay for your education, because you have earned it. I want to do that for you, but you need to understand that it is my choice, not your entitlement. Do you understand the difference?"

Matthew, "Like we shouldn't take it for granted, right?"

"Exactly."

Brett, "Dad, we don't, really. We appreciate the life we have. And we know you work hard to provide it for us."

Kelsey, "We love you Daddy."

You see, my kids got it. If my wife would respond to me this way once in a while and basically agree with everything I said, our marriage would be so much less volatile.

Bill Night became something that I refreshed more with individual bills than a comprehensive lecture about all bills in a single sitting again. In the winter when the public service bill came, I would ask, "Who wants to guess how much it cost to heat the house in January?" Cell phone bills were always fun to go over. We would also play guess the bill every time we ate out for a meal. The objective of the financial lectures was to get the kids thinking about how much it cost to live in what I always referred to as this great country of ours.

REAL WORLD LECTURE # 3
COUNTRY

I apologize to any one who leans left politically and instinctively dislikes people with certain conservative views. I proudly admit that I have a few such views, and some do appear in this section. This book is not intended to be political in any way shape or form, however, in speaking to the kids about the history of the country they called home, it was impossible not to let some of my political views come through.

In a healthy juxtaposition Julie would sometimes act as counter balance to certain of my right leaning opinions that she didn't necessarily agree with. It is amazing to me to see the passion with which today's journalists deny that their reporting of the news ever reflects their personal opinions. This is just not a credible position to take. If you have a view, it stands to reason that it comes through when the subject is political, and I admit that was the case when I discussed country with my children.

Neither Julie nor I had an agenda for the kids beyond being happy and independent in their adult lives, so it was easy to discuss politics and the country openly and to encourage debate and feedback. Like religion, their ultimate interest in history and political affairs would be a personal journey that Julie and I had little control over.

When the kids were young, the simple point of this lecture was that the kids were lucky to be born in the United States of America because it is the greatest country on the face of the earth. I always figured that this is the way most Dad's talked to their kids about their country. I assumed that Dads in the UK, Canada, Australia, India, Germany, Israel, Japan, France etc. also believed that their country is the greatest on the face of the earth. What I mean is that if you have been lucky enough to live a good productive life, surrounded by family and friends who love and care about you, the *place* where you lived that life must be the greatest place on the face of the earth. At least that is the way I have always looked at my country. I just felt lucky to be here, you know with the whole freedom and liberty thing going for us.

So, at home when the kids were younger, I was a cheerleader for America and had a goal of raising kids who loved their country and had a sense of what had come before them. I would make the main point about how lucky they were to be born in the U.S. and then I would surround it passionately with stuff that was over their head. They didn't care because we were having fun cheerleading for America and I was getting them riled up, which they enjoyed.

This would normally occur on a Sunday night where I was usually tasked with baths and showers while Mom made lunches and cleaned up from the weekend that was about to end. I would start lecturing as they got into their pajamas. I was always overly enthusiastic about country as a subject, and the kids recognized it and played along. I started, "Isn't it great that we are going to get up tomorrow and go be productive in America?"

The kids, "Yeah!"

"I mean, you guys are going to get up and go to school, Daddy is going to go to work, and Mom is going to work in the comfortable nest — just like millions of other families in America. You know the people that get up and go to work or school everyday to improve their lives are the backbone of this country. Without hard workers getting educated and then getting up and doing something productive every day, the economy falters, and the whole country goes straight down the tubes. You three need to keep working hard to get your education so you can get a job when you are about 22 years old. Then you can move out of the comfortable nest, make your own way, and contribute to the United States of America!"

My five-year old daughter, "I don't want to leave you, Daddy."

To Kelsey I replied softly, "Then you don't ever have to leave me, sweetheart." To the boys harshly, "But you two guys are out of here and working in about 15 years."

Julie leaned her head in from the other room, and said, "Ted. They are 10, 8, and 5. They don't need the working-class hero speech yet."

I continued, ignoring Julie. "You need to hear this because you guys are the future. You three, and tens of millions of others just like you sitting at home with their parents right now, getting ready for school tomorrow – you guys are the future of this country. You need to appreciate what it means to be a part of this great country. Do you understand what I am saying?"

They nodded in the affirmative, and convincingly so. It was funny how when I got going on America I preached, and the kids reacted more militarily. "Good, because right now and for like the next 15 years your job is to be a good kid, get a good education, and stay out of trouble so you can prepare for the real world when you are an adult. Then it is time to go to work, like Daddy does every day. You got it?"

All three loudly, "Yes sir!"

These rants always needed to be reasonably short, as the kids were still at short attention span theatre stage. Julie predictably would show up about this time to stare at me and say, "Honey? They are children. Please stop this nonsense and turn on America's Funniest Home Videos."

The kids all rebelled in unison. "Yeah! We want America's Funniest Home Videos!"

I relented, but still managed to make one last point. "Of course, we can watch *AMERICA'S* Funniest Home videos, because we live in *AMERICA* and are free to do whatever we want to do!" Looking at the kids and prepping them, "Tell me about America?"

In unison, "It is the greatest country in the world!"

I looked smugly at their Mom, "See, they are getting it." On went the television and we were done.

Okay, so I'm an unabashed homer. However, there is certainly an argument to be made about how fortunate we are to live in America and I made it to my children often. Frankly, I am stunned that there is any argument at all, especially within the country itself. Despite our

102

past and expected future missteps (being the leader of the free world has a lot of responsibility attached to it), there has never been any question in my mind that the intentions of my country are honorable and that we stand for the advancement of freedom, peace, and human rights throughout the world. As the kids got older, I wanted them to understand this and be proud of their country.

After September 11, 2001, the lectures and dialogue about country obviously took on greater significance for my awakened children. They were 19, 17, and 14 when we were hit on September 11, and they wanted to understand how and why this had happened. We talked a lot about this together as a family, as I am sure millions of other families did after the attack.

Watching the Blame America crowd put the cause of 9/11 squarely on our own backs, I wondered how parents in those homes presented America to their kids. I mean, it has to be difficult to raise kids in America when deep down you think that the country sucks. At what age do you begin telling your kids that the team they play for is a loser, a bully, a racist, and the cause of most of the world's problems? At what age do you start telling your kids that the current President of the United States is a bigger terrorist than Bin Laden or Sadaam – with no absolutely facts to support the opinion?

Things have certainly changed from when I was a kid when it comes to respecting the office of the President. I was brought up to respect the Presidency because we – the entire country – had voted and been heard. My Dad would say, "This President (whoever he is) was elected by a vote of the people and we need to salute him and support him because the office itself stands for something much greater than the man occupying it."

When I was in my late teens and Dad was concerned about my general lack of any true motivation, he pointed out what he saw as a disturbing political trend. "The biggest fear I have is that someday the people who believe they can vote themselves a paycheck may outnumber the people who believe that hard work and productivity is what drives the American Dream. If that scale ever actually tips, we are in big trouble. You need to develop a better work ethic, so you don't become part of the problem." Dad always tied any big picture political commentary back to his own children.

I remember when I talked to my Dad about the first Presidential election that I was eligible to vote in. This was 1976, the Jimmy Carter/Gerald Ford election, and I was in college at Auburn where there was plenty of dialogue on campus about Carter, who was from nearby Plains, Georgia. It became clear to me that Carter didn't stand for much of anything that I believed in. When President Carter won, I lamented about this to my Dad and he responded by pitching the bigger picture.

"If President Carter turns out to be as bad as you and I think he is, then the voters will vote him out in four years. No single person can destroy this great country in four years, even as President. There are too many checks and balances." He continued, "Within this country, we elect our leaders, and they lead us. If we don't like the direction they are taking us as a nation, we change leadership through the voting process. As different as we are and as divided as we seem, it is always amazing to watch how we pull together and put politics aside when the stakes really matter." My Dad was remembering the way we had pulled together in World War II, a fight he had been a part of.

A few years later when President Carter's response to the Soviets rolling tanks into Afghanistan was to boycott the summer Olympics my Dad told me, "This President is done. He will not be re-elected because he is too weak at a serious time for our country."

Although Dad turned out to be right and a stronger President was elected by an electoral landslide in 1980, we were both very confused as we watched President Reagan face partisan Democrat and media opposition every step of the way as he confronted Communism in the 1980s. The way we stood together as a country seemed to be changing, even when the stakes really mattered.

When we were hit on 9/11 my real-world conversations with the kids got serious. This was a war that could conceivably go on for a large portion of their lives. My view was that we were at war with radical Islam and our responses to over two decades of attacks had been muted at best. Now we had been hit at home (actually for the second time in 10 years including the first World Trade Center bombing in 1992). In my mind this was a war that would be not unlike the Cold War in terms of length. Patience would be required, which is always a problem for America. I wanted the kids to understand the stakes and how we would respond as a country.

So, on the evening of September 11, 2001 I optimistically made the same basic point to my kids that my Dad had made to me many years earlier. "This is a tragic day for all Americans. However, I want you to watch how we rally as a country around this unprovoked attack. Much of what has happened since the hostages were taken in Iran in the late 1970s has been out of sight and out of mind for many Americans, but you need to know that we have been attacked by Islamic extremists in our foreign embassies and other places where Americans live abroad for over 20 years. After 9/11, it will be clear to everyone that we are at war with radical Islam. This is a wake-up call for all Americans. Watch how we pull together and put politics aside over the next few years. We will do whatever it takes, for however long it takes, and we will all be on the same basic page."

My kids have watched how things have played out and are as confused as my Dad and I were in the 1980s. After watching much of the media coverage in the months that followed the worst attack on American soil in history, Matthew once asked me, "Dad, can you explain how anyone is acting like we are the bad guys in all this?" Of course, I couldn't.

The real-world lectures marked the beginning of adulthood, where we talked more and more about things in an interactive way rather than a one-sided lecture. The kids had questions and I had some answers – but not all the answers. They still turned to their mother when they wanted all the answers and of course, as a true Democrat, she pretended to have them.

HAPPY HOLIDAYS FROM THE HENDERSONS

When I compare the content of past Henderson holiday letters with others that we receive each year, it becomes painfully obvious to me that I don't share enough information about our lives in our letter. Many of the holiday letters we receive, thoughtfully share intimate details of how individual family members have worked each year to help make the world a better place in which to live. It makes me feel a little insecure that, because of the superficial nature of my holiday letters, many of you may see our lives as pretty insignificant and shallow by comparison. The reality is that we are a very accomplished family and I'm proud of our achievements, I've just held back in order to go for some laughs in our letter. So, I'd like to get a little serious this year and take time to salute the Henderson's on a great 2003.

Julie, while volunteering in Kelsey's high school chemistry class this past October, discovered a new element. Look for JULINHIUM (Symbol Jh) on your new periodic tables in '04. We are really proud of her, of course, and are keeping our fingers crossed about that Nobel thing next December. Early tests are indicating that JULINHIUM, when combined with ARGON and COBALT, may cure AIDS. We are happy for the possible breakthrough, not for the personal acclaim that may accompany it, but for the good it will do mankind. Great job, honey!!

Ted, unbeknownst to everyone, has been in on the development of Viagra since the early 1980s. It seems that he is one of 1,184 males in the world who secrete an enzyme critical to Viagra's effectiveness with improved potency. Can you believe how lucky Julie is?

Brett (21 and about to graduate from CSU with a finance/marketing degree) has job offers from every Fortune 500 company but is more likely to reach out and help others. Since her death in 1997, the Pope has been after Brett to take Mother Teresa's place as a comforting global presence – and Brett isn't even Catholic! At this point, Brett seems inclined to acquiesce to John Paul II's wishes, sacrificing money for the betterment of humankind, just the way we taught him. We are proud of you!

Matthew (19, a sophomore accounting major at CSU) is also a Navy SEAL and has political aspirations. The Republican Party has identified Matthew as "their guy" for 2032 and are already grooming him for the Presidency. They like the balance of his intelligence, his calm demeanor, and his 11 kills in international conflict. I'd like to be humble and say we didn't see this coming, but we did. We knew Matthew was Presidential material ever since Julie and I identified him as "gifted and talented" in 1986 when he became potty trained. I am looking forward to lower taxes in 2032 Matthew, I mean Mr. President!

Kelsey (16 and a sophomore in high school) has found getting her drivers license to be no big deal. This is because a few years ago we discovered that Kelsey can fly. I don't mean airplanes. Two years ago, she simply levitated and started to fly. We are so proud of her for having a super power --- and for a 16-year-old, she is handling it really well. We have visited the White House a few times to discuss potential military applications. It seems the Defense Department is interested in basing their newest fighter on Kelsey's unique aerodynamic characteristics. If they do, they'll call it the 'KelStealth'. Thanks for helping protect America, honey!

I'm so glad that we could share our accomplishments and achievements with you this year and wrap it in the veil of a holiday greeting.

Love, Ted, Julie, Brett, Matthew and Kelsey

P.S. In real news Ginger the bulldog, now 5, just became house trained. She is not the sharpest tool in the shed but remains very cute and lovable.

CHAPTER 7
SHOWING UP AS DAD

Among the three tangible ways I would attempt to do my job, showing up as Dad was my favorite, especially when the kids were younger, and I was still Daddy. This role played out in the evenings after work, on weekends and holidays, and from the road when I called home at night while traveling on business. This part of my responsibility often took place in the comfortable nest or on vacation, where first priorities were about enjoying our time together as a family. That fact lifted this post to the top of the showing up triumvirate.

For over 25 years, showing up as Dad has been the best – holding them in my arms, rocking them to sleep, walks in the stroller, playing chase games on my knees, holding a little hand everywhere we went, carrying a tired one on my shoulders, messy meals in the high chair, watching them learn to walk and talk, potty training, band-aiding a scraped knee, and capturing all three in my arms when I got home from work every day.

More, there were Christmas mornings, reading stories before bed, saying prayers together, helping with homework, watching them play with friends, teaching them to swim in pools and then in the ocean, teaching them to ride a bike, playing board games and card games, playing catch, rebounding, watching a school or church concert, and screaming together on a rollercoaster.

More, spending time lighting fireworks together on the 4th, teaching them how to drive a car, watching as they fell in love for the first time, watching them stumble and fall, watching them pick themselves up, high school graduation, college graduation, laughing together, crying together, and being able to get a hug and a kiss almost every day from each child for around 18 years. All I had to do was show up as Dad and I got all this in return. What a deal.

While I loved every moment of it, showing up as Dad eventually got to the kids a little bit. I readily admit that my personality is such that I have a tendency to beat everything to death, and that I was most prolific in this regard when lecturing my kids about almost anything. "Dad, we asked what time it was, not for the history of timepieces." As they got older and were encouraged to challenge me respectfully with logical arguments, the one they made most frequently was that I had to stop it with the lectures.

As Matthew once said, "You never stop, Dad. You're like the Energizer Bunny. I mean, I am eating a bowl of cereal, minding my own business and you go with, 'You know life can be a lot like a bowl of cereal.' Dad stop it. Life isn't like a bowl of cereal at all. You just make up some lecture about 'how milk, sugar, and cereal have to learn to live together in the balanced bowl of life' or something like that. It is just way too much. Please stop. I'm just trying to eat here."

Or Brett, "Dad, please, we have been talking about this for almost half an hour. I know that when I use the blender to make a milkshake I have to clean up after myself. I understand that with the right to use the blender comes the responsibility to clean up the blender. I understand that if I don't take that responsibility, I could lose blender privileges as a consequence of my actions. I get it. Don't you think this is overkill?"

Or Kelsey recently, "Daddy, I am showing up as your daughter and asking you nicely. You need to stop. You have made it very clear to me that boys are smelly, sweaty, and interested in one thing. I get it. Now please stop telling me this ten times a day."

When they made fun of me like this it was clear that the lecture approach, though probably overdone, was working. I would hear these complaints and be thinking, "Balanced bowl of life? Loss of blender privileges? Boys are interested in one thing? Awesome, these kids have been listening to me."

While I knew that I was probably going overboard, I told the kids that I was not going to stop with the lectures. "I have only 18 years to make sure you understand how things work so you can move forward independently. You kids keep making enough bonehead moves that I'm not sure you're out of the woods yet. The lectures are my insurance policy. By the way, in the real world, you need to understand how an insurance policy works. First, don't ever buy life insurance until someone is counting on you. Second, insurance protects you against..." Yes, I was the Energizer Bunny.

The volume of lectures accelerated as the kids got older because the disciplinary lecture took the place of time-outs and spankings as consequences of questionable behavior. Showing up as Dad included discipline and yes, I've admitted it, when they were younger, I sometimes spanked my kids - call the authorities.

With my young kids, spankings were reserved only for major issues - like going into the street. When the kids were young, we lived in a house that sat on a fairly busy street corner. Although the kids were too young for a staying alive lecture, I recognized the busy street for what it was - the possible life altering big mistake. Of course, a young child would never recognize that unless someone made it very clear to them. Enter Dad.

It was my job to make sure that they understood the street was a "BIG NO, NO" and I determined that a whack on their diapered butt when the ventured into the street alone was the best way to get that point across. I viewed the spanking in this case as the equivalent of the electric shock dog collar that defines the yard for a dog. This tactic worked, and my young kids always stopped at the curb and looked for Mommy or Daddy to take their hand before they would ever step foot in the street. Mission accomplished, and, in my opinion, sometimes the ends justified the means.

I also have proof that spankings do sometimes work when all else fails. At the age of four, Kelsey went through a period when she was biting everyone, even the dog. For any parent who has dealt with this issue, you know that it is tough behavior to stop once it starts. We tried everything from time outs, to loss of privileges, to spankings. Even my "Stop the madness" biting lectures fell on deaf four-year-old ears. Nothing worked. In fact, it was getting worse – she even bit Mom. We were actually considering taking some questionable guidance from another parent who advised us to "Bite the child back." I wasn't there yet.

In the midst of this I came home one night after a softball game, put the boys in front of the television and bounded upstairs to see what

Julie and Kelsey were up to. Kelsey had just finished her bath and was hanging out with Mom wearing her cute little girl summer night gown. As always, she was thrilled to see her Daddy, and as I sat down on the bath tub step Kelsey hugged me and climbed on me. Always cool. At some point, her head found my lap and she was just rolling her head from my knee to my thigh while Julie and I talked.

Suddenly, I felt this excruciating pain as my daughter bit through my thin sweat pants into a meaty part of my leg just above my knee. I reacted without thinking and brought my hand down hard on her thinly covered thigh – a loud SLAP pierced the room. I had essentially spanked my daughter on her thigh. Kelsey stopped biting me immediately, so she could start screaming about how much her thigh hurt. Julie stared at me and I tried to explain my actions by showing her where Kelsey had bit me. Note to husbands - you lose in this situation.

As I look back, I don't know how I could have reacted any differently. The pain from her bite was so unexpected that I just instinctively slapped down, and then it was over. It took us about three weeks to realize that my daughter's biting behavior had been instantly cured that night. After that night, we never said another word to her about biting and she never bit anyone again. I found that interesting. I think that we would have had to deal with the biting issue for at least another couple of months if lectures and time outs were the only weapons that we used in our parenting arsenal. She was absolutely biting everyone and everything and would not stop – the disciplinary tactics had no impact whatsoever. I was reassured that the spanking had its place.

As the children got older and spankings became obsolete, the disciplinary lecture took their place. As my brother, sister, and I had agreed about 35 years earlier, we sometimes would have preferred for Dad to just haul off and whack us rather than lecture for an hour with that vein popping out of his forehead. Of course, Dad never whacked anyone beyond childhood spankings, but he lectured his heart out. I remembered that my brother and I had agreed that this could be torturous, so when I showed up as Dad to my older kids, the lecture was also used to punish them.

111

Obviously, none of the kids enjoyed being punished, and they voiced their unhappiness differently. Brett urinated behind his dresser. Kelsey once threatened to sue me for abuse after she had received a spanking. Matthew was always less obvious. One time I sent Matthew to his room after we had tried - and failed - to resolve things in conversation. I always reminded the kids that I would treat them as adults if they acted like adults, especially when it came to actions that required discipline. Matthew didn't quite get there in this discussion, so I sent him to his room to contemplate his actions. I would come up about 10 minutes later to further our discussion and see if I could get my point across after he had calmed down.

When I entered his room, he seemed much calmer than when he had stormed upstairs a few minutes earlier yelling, "It's not fair!!" As I began to talk to him, he seemed distracted. He kept looking over towards his wall where his team sports pictures were hanging. Every time we made eye contact, his eyes would trail over to the wall of pictures.

I went on for a few minutes and then I asked him what he thought. He shrugged his shoulders and again glanced over at the team pictures on his wall. This time my eyes followed his and finally I saw it. One of his baseball team pictures was hanging slightly askew. A closer examination revealed that Matthew had spent the ten minutes in his room completely scratching out the face of his coach in the picture – me. I don't mean he just inked my face out, he had angrily scratched out the photo of my entire face so there was this big grey cardboard hole under my hat with some ink on it. It looked pretty funny and I later laughed about how subtle Matthew was compared to Brett and Kelsey in delivering the same message - "I don't like you anymore."

This message was okay with me because it meant that the children were able communicators. Mom and I could communicate too, and the children knew that there were times when we weren't too pleased with them either. Things balanced out. When I was communicating that I wasn't happy through a disciplinary speech, the kids knew that they'd best sit tight and take it. If they sent signals (eye rolls and deep breaths) that indicated they wanted out of the sermon because it was dragging on, I would strike out aggressively. "So, am I boring you here? Because you are looking at me like you are tired of this lecture, which would indicate to me that you understand what I am saying to you. That would stand in direct contradiction to your behavior, which is what triggered this conversation in the first place. You don't get it. So please save me your eye rolls and deep breaths because you aren't going anywhere for a while. Got it? We are going to stay here and talk until I understand what your thought process was in this situation. Do you understand me?"

A resigned, but firm, "Yes sir," would generally follow and the child would sit still and take their punishment in lecture form.

If they weren't in trouble, they begged me to stop lecturing by sending signals, usually the aforementioned eye rolls and deep breaths. Sometimes I missed them. Without question, the clearest signal I ever received that I had lectured too long was the time Brett (then 15) actually flipped me the finger while I was lecturing him.

We both remember that the lecture had gone on for a while and had hit the point where I was repeating myself. Brett wasn't in any trouble and I was just being obnoxious Dad, lecturing educationally about something. I was on a roll and couldn't stop. As the lecture ground on, Brett had sent non-verbal signals and inserted many "Okay, Dad," and "I get it, Dad," comments. As I said, when the kids weren't in any trouble, these signals were usually enough to make me stop. Not this time. As I made another point, Brett had had enough. He shifted in his seat, and out of frustration very clearly flipped me the bird.

Seeing the reaction on his face, there is no question that he was as stunned as I was. This was so out of character for my oldest son that neither of us really knew how to react. He recovered first, "Dad, oh my gosh! I am so sorry. I can't believe that I just did that. Dad, I am so, so sorry. I...I...I don't know what caused me to do that. Can you believe that I just did that?"

I answered slowly, "No, I can't." I was stunned, but also a bit amused. I did recognize that I had been over-lecturing him for about 30 minutes about something he wasn't in trouble for. However, now he was in trouble because no matter how bad my droning address was, his judgment in flipping me off was worse.

I then proceeded to punish my oldest son the best way I knew how. "Brett, I don't know what just happened here, but clearly you lost control and did something that you know is wrong and disrespectful - right to your father's face. I admit I was rambling, but you could have approached me in a better way to make me stop. Humor works, you know that. This is the kind of loss of control that makes drinking and drugs so dangerous. Have you been drinking tonight? I mean you aren't drunk are you?"

He was 15 and had already started to hear the staying alive lecture on drinking. He smiled and said, "No Dad, I am not drunk."

I continued, "Well, that's good. Given what you just did, I had to wonder for a minute because drinking often causes really bad judgment. I want you to remember that you are 15 and that is too young to drink - period. There is no 'Keep it between the fence posts' at age 15 when it comes to drinking – there is only 'no drinking at all because you are too young.' Got it?"

He can see where I am going and settles in for a completely different lecture, "Got it."

I begin, "You are about to hit high school and start driving - lots of serious stuff lies ahead for you, and you need to have good judgment to navigate the bridge to adulthood..." Brett had no choice but to tolerate the disciplinary staying alive lecture as a consequence for flipping off his stunned father.

You know, they don't teach you how to deal with this kind of stuff in the parenting books. There is no chapter entitled, "What to do when a child you love flips you the bird" in any parenting book. Real parents basically deal with a constant barrage of unbelievable situations that are unique to each of their children, on the fly and in real time. There are no trial runs and decisions made on the fly can sometimes backfire.

amazon Gift Receipt

Send a Thank You Note

You can learn more about your gift or start a return here too.

Scan using the Amazon app or visit
http://a.co/2AlCTya

Dad's Top Ten Lectures
Order ID: 111-8163804-9321024 Ordered on May 1, 2019

Sometimes when I showed up as Dad, I had to take charge, make a firm decision, and override even Mom's fervent wishes. I only did this when Julie was being totally irrational, and I was acting as the clear voice of reason. Sometimes it cost me – as in cash. Such was the case one weekend when we decided to take a family trip to the zoo on a beautiful summer day with a young Brett and a younger Matthew.

This day represented a big outing for our family since it was the first time that both boys were diaper free. Brett was completely potty trained and younger brother Matthew was just starting to wear big boy underwear. No diaper bag was required for this trip and Julie and I felt somewhat unchained for the first time in a few years. The boys were pumped for the zoo visit, especially Matthew who was sporting his favorite Scooby Doo underwear under his green shorts.

Matthew absolutely loved his Scooby Doo underwear and we had not been able to get him to wear any other pair in his short-lived 'big boy underwear' career yet. Ever the tolerant Mom, Julie washed his Scooby Doo's about once a day and the result was that the week-old underwear had already shrunk and was a bit tight on young Matthew. This didn't matter to him one bit, as he still chose the tight Scooby Doos over his other assorted underwear choices each and every day.

We thought the zoo was a good destination choice for our first 'no diaper' outing since the zoo had plenty of restrooms around if a sprint to the potty might be required. A sprint was required because Matthew let the excitement get to him and completely dumped in his underwear within a few minutes of being at the zoo. I recognized this immediately - the awkward and always recognizable 'I have a load in my pants' gait was a dead giveaway - and rushed him off to the men's room.

Once inside I was relieved to find that the tight Scooby Doos had captured the problem wholly and the clean up was quite easy and efficient. I proceeded to use the Scooby Doos as if they were a diaper, buried them deep in the paper towel trash, and used wet and dry paper towels to finish the clean up. I briefly lectured Matthew on the joys of 'going commando' and made a big deal about how cool it was, hoping to get his mind off his lost Scooby Doos. He and I came out of the restroom ready to go within about 5 minutes of the accident and I faced a disbelieving Julie. "Wow! That was efficient."

I answered, "Yep. No problemo. Piece of cake. No overflow onto his shorts at all. He is all cleaned up and ready to go."

Brett and Matthew had moved out of ear shot to practice their broad jump and compare their distance to the highlighted animal barometer. I was enjoying watching them, feeling my oats about how efficiently I had solved what could have been a semi-disaster for the day, when Julie hit me with, "So where is his Scooby Doo underwear?"

Uh-oh. I stammered, "I, uh, left them in the trash in the rest room."

She gave me that forlorn motherly look and said, "You can't throw out his favorite underwear, he will be crushed."

I looked at Matthew who was laughing and having a grand time and replied, "He doesn't seem to be missing them at all, and he saw me toss them in the trash."

She was insistent, "Honey, you have to go in there and get them. He will want to know where they are tomorrow, and he might not wear anything else. This could negatively impact the progress we have made with his potty training. You have to go get them for him."

As someone who had just cleaned up a rather substantial mess, I was wondering exactly what progress she was referring to. When I spoke, I was just as insistent, "You have got to be kidding me. I am not going to go fish out his loaded Scooby Doos, clean them in the toilet, and carry them around with me at the zoo all day. I am not going to do that."

"But they are his favorite."

"Not anymore they aren't. Trust me, Scooby is shitfaced, and Matthew has no further interest in them."

"But he will tomorrow, that is my point. Please go get them."

116

I argued, "You have no idea what you are asking me to do. I am telling you the underwear is beyond hope. Even if I wash it out, we will have a soaking wet pair of dirty underwear to deal with for the next two hours. I am not going to deal with that – and neither are you. Let's just have a nice day at the zoo, what do you say?"

She thought for a few minutes and then said, "Maybe we should go through the zoo and then pick them up on our way out?"

I am thinking that I married a complete nut at this point and I play the only card I have left. It is one I know will strike a chord with her given our 'fun on a budget' approach to life with two young children on a single income. In a solemn tone I said to her, "I will pay you $100 to not make me go in there. You can buy Matthew 10 pair of Scooby Doo underwear later today and pocket the difference. How does that sound."

Julie laughed and then saw that I was dead serious. She looked at me skeptically and said, "You are telling me that you would rather pay me $100 than go in there and get his Scooby Doo underwear?"

"That is exactly what I am telling you."

"You don't let us spend that much on dinner out."

"I know. That is how much I don't want to deal with his messed up Scooby Doo underwear right now."

She noodled this and said, "$100, huh?"

"Yep."

She put out her hand and said, "Deal." We shook and enjoyed the rest of the day at the zoo. I paid Julie her $100 when we got home and everyone seemed happy with the outcome. Unfortunately, Matthew found out that he actually liked going commando and we struggled to get him to put on any underwear for about a week. Unintended consequences are always a part of any parenting decision.

Finally, showing up as Dad included my all-out efforts to get a laugh from the kids – at almost any cost. This was a big issue between Julie and me, especially when I would do something that she viewed as totally inappropriate to get a cheap laugh. A prime example was the time I stuffed some Jell-O up my nose at the dinner table and then told the kids to watch as I blew it out my nose to the waiting dog – who caught the 'Jell-O nose shot' in mid air. Gross, I know, but it got a big laugh from all three kids at the time, with one child actually exclaiming "Awesome!" Plus, I personally thought it was hysterical and the dog was happy too. Bulldog Polly and I were three for four in our catch the Jell-O nose shot game – and it *was* awesome. I had a lot of childish stuff like this in my arsenal and I admit that my mindset was often not very adult. "The kids laughed, so I win" was basically how I viewed things. Julie obviously had a different view.

This was what showing up as Dad often meant for me – for all my efforts within the home, I was still frequently in trouble with Julie. My suspect judgment in terms of doing anything for a laugh with the kids was always front and center in our marriage and my wife was rightly concerned that like my Dad, I lacked a bit in the "compassionate" side of my conservatism. She didn't want her kids to become insensitive dolts like she sometimes thought I was.

As Julie and I have lived for 27 years in a "purple" marriage, we recognized that there were subjects on which we had fundamental differences that could impact the kids. As the real-world lectures were in play and politics came up, Mom would often give a different side of the story than what I had presented. In showing up as Dad, I made sure to point out the obvious to the children. "You three are lucky to have such a wonderful, Mom, and I'm lucky to have her as my wife. You know that Mom and Dad look at things differently and have figured out how to make that work in our marriage. Again, humor helps. Mom has your best interests at heart just like I do, so you should always listen to her and consider her input just as I hope you consider mine. She is a smart lady and has a wonderful heart; she is nicer than Dad. Between the two of us, you get to see different views and approaches to things that should strengthen your ability to make decisions as adults."

So, Julie and I, as different as we were, were both committed to showing up as Dad and Mom and celebrating our differences with our children. The perspectives that we brought to the table were not only impacted by our inherent diversity, they were also impacted by the environments in which we spent most of our time. Of course, Mom was nicer, kinder, and gentler than Dad – she spent most of her time in the comfortable nest where she was somewhat protected and loved unconditionally. As a contrast, most of my time was spent in the workplace, where I was not loved unconditionally nor protected.

HAPPY HOLIDAYS FROM THE HENDERSONS

The upcoming New Year is a big year at the Henderson house. We are about to have our first child strike out on his own. A quick, hindsight comment on parenting over a 20+ year period --- while this time of life is wonderful, the early years of parenting are more fun, less stressful and less expensive than the later years. The early years are more fun because you can actually hang out with your kids all the time. The early years are less stressful because the kids are dependent on you for mobility, so there is a sense of control. And the early years are less expensive because I can do the math: the battery powered Jeep they had at 5 years old didn't require premium gas, titanium studded snow tires and collision and liability insurance. While this may be obvious to most, I spell it out because the twilight of my parenting years have been defined by being a provider and dominated by a single question -- "Will the nest ever really empty?" In 2005 we will get our answer.

Incredibly, this will be Brett's (22) last Christmas at home as he will graduate from Colorado State this month (finance and marketing) and move into his own place sometime soon thereafter – the job will dictate when. Accordingly, his Christmas gifts will be on the practical (read: no fun) side this year. Julie proudly showed me a skillet she bought for him on sale --- only to burst into tears because it meant our first child is really leaving home. Just when I thought that my wife had gone over the top crazy, she gathered herself and said through her tears, "I honestly don't think I'll ever be able to cook again. Any skillet will be a painful reminder that Brett isn't home anymore." I must admit, she is good. It is this type of devilish, ingenious, psychotic behavior that has kept me confused and intrigued for 25 years of marriage.

Matthew (20) will take a break from Colorado State and spend 5 months next semester in Australia studying abroad -- see comment above on the later years being more expensive. Nice gig if you can get it. I am stunned that I wasn't enough of a visionary/salesman to get this type of trip out of my parents when I was younger. As the provider I wrote the check for the semester in Australia and took comfort in the fact that Matthew is an accounting major who can sell. There is some evidence in the Henderson home that there is a modest future with that combination. In other words, I am confident that Matthew is on track to leave with his own skillet pretty soon.

Kelsey is 17 (junior in high school) and enjoying the basement penthouse all to herself. She is not enjoying all the focus and attention that being the only one at home brings, but to her credit, she has managed Mom and Dad well. On the rare occasion that she does emerge from her quarters, it is to smile and ask if she can go out to eat with friends – in which case she will need some money; or to smile and ask to go shopping – in which case she will need some money; or to smile and ask if she can order some cell phone accessories on-line – in which case she will need Mom's credit card. While I love her smile, I am happiest when she stays in the basement.

The ongoing focus for Ted is financial and for Julie emotional. This is a tough combination that continues to bring compelling dialogue to the marriage. We are excited about the prospect of beginning a new chapter in our life while watching the kids move forward independently. Eventually, this letter will be about Julie and me and all the exciting things we are doing and how good we look and feel. The good news is that as time goes on, there will be more room for exciting stuff about Ginger. The bulldog is pumped! We hope this finds our friends and family healthy, happy and blessed.

Merry Christmas and Happy New Year 2005!
Love, Ted, Julie, Brett, Matthew, and Kelsey

CHAPTER 8
SHOWING UP AS PROVIDER

Showing up as the provider was the function that least involved lectures to my children; I was too busy working. While I primarily viewed myself as Dad, like most fathers I spent more time at work than at home, averaging 60-80 hour work weeks over a 28-year business career. I have been lucky to stumble through a career that has been interesting, rewarding, and challenging, and luckier still to have worked for people who accommodated my desire to be a good Dad.

According to the World Book Encyclopedia, the provider "Gives what is needed or wanted; arranges to supply means of support; and takes care for the future." I did all that, but I viewed it a bit more simply. I thought of myself as the provider this way: "I am a good dog who is willing to go fetch. When I get home, I just need to be petted and told that I have been a good dog and then I will go fetch some more tomorrow."

When the kids were younger, this was easy - they greeted me like the returning king everyday when I got home from work. This would never fail to re-energize me, and I would happily go fetch again the next day. As the kids got older and busier with their own lives, I still arrived home from work exhausted and looking to be petted, but it was no longer that big of a deal to my busy children. Thankfully, it was still a big deal to the dog.

I have to say that the only one who has consistently greeted me the way I want (and need) to be greeted when I get home from work is the dog. She appreciates me, I think, because I am a good dog like she is. We can relate to each other. She understands simple things like, "Dad is the guy who carries in the big bag of dog food and therefore I worship him" or "I poop in the yard, and Dad picks it up. I love this guy." As I have worn down in the twilight of my providing years and the kids have disappeared, it has been the bulldog's attention and unconditional love that have often kept me going. So here is an official shout out to the sixth member of our family over the years, the dog. Thank you Ginger and Polly for the way you have treated me over the years. Humans could learn a lot from dogs on how to make a guy feel unconditionally loved.

Providing is the last part of being a Dad that stops. I stopped showing up as coach as soon as the kids hit high school. Once they could drive, I saw them less and less in the comfortable nest so my ability to show up as Dad slowed also. But showing up as the provider? That function has never slowed and I'm still doing it with Kelsey in college.

I have heard motivational speakers preach that in order to be happy in your career you should first "Find your passion and then find a job that fits that passion." I have often laughed about this, because for me, it was a complete joke. When I was in my late twenties, I already had a family that was counting on me and I was focused on trying to meet a rapidly increasing monthly nut. Going for your passion professionally may sound inspiring, but there is a time and a place for everything and this was not the time for me. I had a career going that could support the family if I hung in there. So, I kept my head down and pushed forward with a career that was interesting and supported a comfortable life style but was hardly a passion. Passion was reserved for my family.

Work wasn't my life, and none of my jobs have ever defined me. What I did productively during the day simply allowed me to fund the life we wanted to live as a family. I took it for granted that I would be the sole income for our family, just like my Dad had done. Providing was, amazingly, something that I *didn't* worry about early in our marriage; I worried about everything else as a parent, but not work. So, when Julie got pregnant, I told her that it was no problem for her and the coming kids to "Hop on my back" and I'd handle everything financially. I was 25 at the time and, need I remind everyone again, completely clueless.

Five years later at age 30 our family was complete with Kelsey's arrival and I reiterated my strength, "I'm surprised. Babies don't really cost that much. I am still going strong and we are actually saving some money every month. This is easy."

I was still boastfully confident five years later, "I'm 35 and not even winded. I am rock solid. Hop on board and I'll carry us all the way to the finish line."

At 40, after 15 years of providing, my tires got a bit wobbly, "I am hanging in there; I can definitely make it. I'm a little tired. Do the kids really need so many clothes? Do you think they are considering an in-state college?"

At 45 I started to leak some oil which showed up through some bitching and moaning to Julie. "I am about to be financing and insuring a fleet of five cars! The kids seem healthy, how can their dental and medical bills possibly be this high – after insurance? College books cost how much? How can we possibly spend this much on food and clothes every month? Why won't anyone turn out the lights when they leave a room?"

Now at nearly 50 years old, after 25 years as a provider, I realize that I only made it through the last five years because of a false finish line - the empty nest. I crossed it running on fumes in August saying to Julie, "We are going to spend less in 2006 than we spent in 2005. This is going to be the first time that has happened in over a quarter of a century. I think I'm going to cry."

Looking back, it is unbelievable to me that I have already been a provider for over 25 years. I know my Dad is stunned and amazed. Like most everything else in my life I started stumbling towards my career without a clue, and my Dad was involved. At dinner one night when I was a senior in high school, he asked me, "Have you given anymore thought to what you want to major in?"

I responded with teenage brevity, "No."

Mom then asked me if I had any homework. I told her that I had none and she pushed back, "Honey, it doesn't seem like you are having much homework. Are you staying on top of things? How are your grades?"

Somewhat annoyed, again teenager, I said, "Mom, you know that my grades are good, and I have been accepted at a lot of schools, so it doesn't even matter anymore." I paused and then remembered, "Oh, here you go. I got an accounting test back today and made 100%. How's that? I am killing that class."

My Dad's ears perked up and he said, "There you go. You should major in accounting at college. That's perfect - (grandly) *the language of business.* You couldn't have a better background than accounting if you are interested in business. Do you like the course?"

I said, "Yeah, I guess so. I like that you know if your answer is right because stuff balances out. I mean, I *know* I have the right answers when I turn in my test and that is kind of cool. We have had three tests and I have only missed two points."

My Dad now pushed, "Then you should definitely start out in accounting, so you have some direction. Talk about a great path. This is perfect." He paused and then again said majestically, "*The Language of Business.*" Another pause then, "I am telling you this is perfect. You are good at math. You kind of like the accounting course you are taking. That is all you are looking for when you start college, some direction. If you change your mind and don't like it, you make that move later. This gives you a direction and a place to start. Accounting. This is perfect."

I was thinking that Dad and 'accounting' should get a room. However, I certainly didn't have a better idea, so I declared accounting as my major when I got to college. That relatively arbitrary decision was the first step in my stumble through what would turn out to be a pretty interesting career that supported our family for 28 years.

Truth be told, my Dad worried about my long-term job prospects because I didn't like to work very much when I was a kid. Alert the media – a teenage kid who didn't really like to work. Yep, that was me. I could find any excuse to get out of doing something, and it frustrated my Dad to no end, especially when it came to his own company.

For a long time, I managed to avoid working for my Dad's brick masonry company since construction work was hard and started very early. I figured, "Why would I want to do that?" The first year that I was to work for Dad was after my junior year in high school. But my high school basketball coach convinced him that if I worked hard all summer on my game, I could possibly earn a scholarship to play in college. Dad was great about this and allowed me the summer off to practice, which I did. I was interested in basketball, so my work ethic was solid.

The next summer after my senior year I got mono and couldn't work construction on Doctor's orders – but it was okay for me to relax and hang out at the pool with the girls. This drove Dad nuts, but I had earned a four-year scholarship, so that helped his mood.

Finally, the summer after my freshman year in college arrived and I had no excuses not to work for him. I had been home from college for a few days and I was scheduled to start on Monday. However, I had a softball game on Sunday night - the big 16" Chicago style softball, with no mitts – and fate again intervened. I was playing first base and I scooped a short hop throw from the shortstop, exposing my left hand to the runner who was coming hard down the first base line. I got kicked accidentally and my thumb was broken and dislocated. I went home, called Mom downstairs, showed her my thumb, and asked her if she would take me to the emergency room. I wasn't feeling too well and was getting kind of nauseous.

She said, "Sure honey. I'll go get the car, while you go upstairs and tell Dad what happened. You can't work tomorrow and he needs to know that."

I gave her my best whining "Mom, can you please tell Dad..." look. She would have none of it, pointed upstairs and said, "Go talk to your Dad."

I went up to Dad, who was in bed reading, and showed him my thumb. It was pretty ugly and I told him what had happened. He took a deep breath and the only thing he said was, "I guess it is just not in the cards for you to ever have to work."

Now there is the compassion that I was looking for. Not a word about my thumb, which was hanging at a very awkward angle. Again,

126

Dad could be a tough cookie when he worried about his kids and he was concerned that I would never develop a work ethic because I had hardly worked as a teenager. This made him fret about my long-term prospects. As a parent myself, I know now that he was also concerned that he may have to support me forever.

Okay, so I was a bit of a slacker as a kid. Truth be told, I did understand that Dad worked hard for our family and that I would eventually have to work to provide for myself. I just didn't see the point while I was in high school. When I focused on something that I was interested in, like grades or basketball, I had a good work ethic. Chores and stuff like that just didn't ever interest me so I fought hard to get out of doing them. Dad worried that I had no work ethic and might never leave the comfortable nest. He did have some history to lean on.

For example, I was a paperboy. This was not a long-term job, as my Dad got tired of driving me around to deliver the papers after I had overslept on most mornings. The reason I quit as a paperboy was because my *Dad* couldn't take it any more. I thought that I showed an understanding of the job when I did manage to hang on long enough to get through Christmas and receive the accompanying tips.

There was an interesting foundation lesson here and Dad made sure to point it out to me. "When it comes to work, you have to show up every day. Sometimes you show up and work hard and you get nothing in return. Sometimes you show up and do almost nothing – like you as a paperboy – and still manage to get paid. The lesson here is to keep showing up. I mean, you are probably the worst paperboy that has ever delivered the Chicago Tribune. Your average delivery time is probably around 7:30 a.m. for the three months that you held the job. That is pathetic. However, you hung in there and actually got yourself out of bed for one month and did the job reasonably well. That month happened to be December, and you got paid because Christmas tips are blindly put into envelopes for the carriers. No one would ever really tip you based on your three months of service."

In addition to labeling me the worst paperboy the Chicago Tribune ever employed, Dad also labeled me the worst employee Hodsco Construction (his company) ever had. I only worked for him for two summers and Dad recently reminded me of how embarrassed he was when one of his foremen said to him, "Your son Ted is bad for morale. He is constantly praying for rain. He actually led the men in a rain dance the other day."

I knew this much about construction - if it rained hard enough, construction work was finished for the day and I could go back home and crawl into bed. So, at coffee break, I always turned west and did an impromptu rain dance if the skies were at all threatening. The guys on the crew thought it was funny. Dad didn't and sat me down to explain some business basics to me. "I am running a business here and it supports our family. You need to understand that if it rains, I lose a day of production and it costs me money. Rain is not good for business and my own son is openly praying for rain in front of men that I employ. You look like you don't care about the business when you act like that. You are a representation of me out there and I expect you to act appropriately. Work hard, earn your day's pay and come home. No more rain dances. I want you to quit trying to get out of doing work and actually do some work."

Interestingly, there was one summer when my efforts to get out of work actually gave my Dad hope that I wouldn't be a complete failure. When I was younger my summer job was to mow our lawn. Here again I was the worst lawn mower in the world, but this time with good reason. Simply put, I was deathly afraid of bees. Our suburban Chicago yard had a ton of bees which made mowing the lawn a really bad fit for me job wise. To this day I am afraid of bees and still overreact whenever a bee is around. I start flailing my arms all around my space and then I run away as if I am on fire. People always ask Julie under their breath, "Wow. Is he allergic?"

Ever the supportive wife, Julie says, "No, he's not. It's pathetic, isn't it?"

Anyway, I was about 13 and Dad paid me $10 a week to mow the lawn. There were bees all over our yard and I didn't want to mow. So, I paid our 10-year-old next door neighbor $5 a week to mow it for me. Dad went nuts when he came home early one day, and I was shooting hoops in the driveway with a friend while our neighbor was mowing our lawn. As a consequence, more chores that I didn't do too well were tacked on to my other duties around the house.

I found out later that Dad had said to Mom that night, "Actually, I love what he did here from a business standpoint. For the first time, I think this kid might have a future after all. Bottom line is that his job was to get the lawn mowed. He figured out a way to get the job done while he did something else he wanted to do - and he still pocketed $5. There may be some hope here yet."

The fact that Dad worried about my work ethic and that I might never leave the comfortable nest caused him to show up and take an active interest in my future. Accordingly, he was alert at dinner that spring evening of my senior year to direct me towards accounting in college. I have found that parenting is cool that way. If you just show up, opportunities arise where you can help and direct your kids.

So, Dad showed up and helped direct me to major in accounting at college. I graduated from Auburn in 1979 and my grades were good enough that I got a job with a Big 8 accounting firm in Denver. I had some money in the bank, I had a job, and I owed nobody a dime, so life was good. I had also fallen in love and gotten married.

The first four-years of my career were spent with Arthur Andersen in the audit division. I was exposed to many industries including oil and gas, banking, coal mining, manufacturing, and cable television. I had watched many associates go to work for industry clients over the years and, since I wasn't in love with public accounting, it became clear to me that I was going to move away from Arthur Andersen eventually.

I was most enamored by the cable television industry for the simple, non-business reason that I was addicted to ESPN's emerging coverage of the NCAA basketball tournament's early round games. In other words, I liked the cable industry as a possible career path, because I loved cable as a consumer. I had critical cable industry experience from working on the audit at United Cable Television.

That industry experience landed me a job at Jones Intercable a month before Matthew was born in February 1984. This was the first real decision that I faced in my professional life and I look back with amusement about how much of a risk I thought I was taking leaving public accounting and going into the cable business in the early 1980s in Denver. Jones flourished along with the entire cable industry and was eventually bought out by Comcast; Arthur Andersen no longer exists. It is better to be lucky than good.

My years at Jones overlapped with many of the years when I was coaching, and I will forever be grateful to my bosses for understanding my desire to be a good Dad and allowing me to coach. I walked out in the middle of many serious business meetings because there were thirteen 10-year-olds waiting for me at the baseball field. During this critical time for my kids, I was very lucky to be part of a Jones corporate family that understood family.

Going to work for Jones and aligning myself with the growing cable industry was a decision that would define my career for the next 20+ years. In 1984, through no planning whatsoever, I had stumbled into a growing industry in Denver, a market that was to become known as the U.S. cable capital throughout the 1980's and 1990's. I would stay at Jones from 1984 through 1996 and then become a Wall Street analyst where my focus would be, naturally, the cable industry. I would do the Wall Street thing for about a decade before quitting in May 2006 to re-assess my life and write this book.

The best part of showing up as the provider over the years has been that I could heroically rescue the family from some bad situations if I was willing to step up and write the check. The best example of this is the chronicle of our first bulldog, Polly. The Polly that is referred to in one of the Christmas letters was actually the *second* Polly. The account of the first Polly is a provider story because I was initially trying to get off on the cheap in buying a family dog. The result was a complete disaster.

Kelsey was 6 and had just been officially diagnosed with epilepsy after having seizures since she was 3. She was still a bit young to understand the true impact the diagnosis would have on her life and the fact that she wasn't going to grow out of these seizures. After we left the doctor's office, Julie and I held our tears for later and told Kelsey that we loved her and were proud of the way she had handled herself through a couple of weeks of hospital tests. We then dropped the big parental no-no of saying she could have anything, absolutely anything she wanted as a reward for being such a trooper.

She didn't hesitate, "I want a puppy." Done deal, we were getting a puppy that weekend. Over the last 13 years, this has become a joke within our family as Kelsey teasingly plays Daddy's girl and asks for a puppy whenever she has had a tough time. When the family reconvened that night, we discussed the type of puppy we would get, and an English bulldog was the unanimous choice. The next morning, Saturday, I went to the paper and was thrilled to see that there were three ads for English bulldog puppies. All three ads said, "AKC registered pure bred, English bulldog puppies, 6-8 weeks old". As Julie and I looked together, we noticed that two of the ads had $1,200 prices and the third had a $600 price. I was a bit taken aback at the prices and I said to Julie, "Did you know they were this expensive? (No) What about the discrepancy in price? (Shrug) How can this be? (Shrug, again) We have to at least go take a look at the $600 puppies, don't we?"

Finally, she said, "Sure, can't hurt. There has to be some explanation for the price discrepancy."

I called the number and a woman answered, "Hello?"

I waded in, "Yes Ma'am, I am calling about the ad for the bulldog puppies in the paper. Do you have any left?"

She sounded like I would expect Ma Barker to sound, "Yes, we have two left from a litter of seven, but I have two people coming out to look at them later. Did you want to try to come out and see them before that?"

I shrugged my shoulders while looking at Julie and said, "Sure. Where are you located?"

She gave me the directions and after we hung up, I realized I had forgotten to ask about the price discrepancy. I would do it when we got there. (Bad plan.) We piled the three kids into the car and made the 35-minute drive to where the $600 puppies lived. We arrived at the trailer park community, found the right one and were greeted at the door by what looked like the mother and pirate son from the kid's movie classic, *The Goonies*. The pirate hat worn by the messed-up kid in *The Goonies*, was replaced by a 1930s leather football helmet on this 20 something year-old kid. All my instincts were telling me to get out of there, but the lady asked if we were The Hendersons and I robotically replied, "Yes, we are."

She pointed us to some chairs in the small yard and said, "Why don't you have a seat and we'll bring out the puppies."

A few moments later, out came the son, Brad, holding the two puppies. Brad's shoes were on the wrong feet. He set the puppies down and they proceeded to do what puppies do - they were playful and very cute and immediately bonded with my children. One was a solid tan color and the other a brindle that Matthew fell completely in love with. The tan one had a blood-filled bubble below his right eye and there was nothing apparently wrong with the one that all three of my kids were now playing with. She was adorable. I had assumed this might happen, that the kids would fall for the first puppy they saw, and it was fine with me if that dog cost $600 versus $1,200. What a shrewd Dad I was, making it happen for the kids while still keeping an eye on our family finances.

The kids continued to play with the puppy as I asked the key question, "I couldn't help but notice that the $600 price is half that of the other bulldog puppies advertised in the paper. Why is that? Is there anything wrong with these puppies? What about the tans one's eye?"

She said, "The difference in price is because you will have to take both of these dogs to the vet. The tan one has an eye infection, and we can give you some cream, but you will have to go to a vet for that. Also, the one your kids are playing with has a hemorrhoid problem and is experiencing some diarrhea. I have certificates of health on both dogs from our vet, but you will need to take either one of them to your own vet and get them checked out. That is why we are not asking as much. They have had all their shots and stuff. We have that documentation, don't we Brad?"

Brad is biting his fingernails on fingers that look like they have been kneading dog poop all morning. He replied, "Yup."

The kids have fallen completely for the puppy – already named Polly – and I made the fatal mistake of believing these people and taking a chance that my vet bills will be less than $600. Polly acted and looked fine, except for a swollen behind explained by the hemorrhoid. I wrote the check and signed all the papers and we piled into the car with the puppy and happily drove off.

We got home and played with the puppy for a few hours. We immediately found ourselves dealing with housebreaking because it seemed like pee and poop were literally falling out her as she walked around. The kids didn't really care, because this was truly the sweetest puppy you could ever imagine.

Monday arrived, and I took Polly to the vet. I explained the hemorrhoid issue that we were apparently dealing with and commented about the very frequent stream of eliminations that emanated from her. The vet performed a few basic tests as he would of any 7-week-old puppy and pronounced her in good health and very cute and sweet. Then he said, "Let's see what the problem is back here."

He pulled on a glove, lubed his index finger, and proceeded to drive it three knuckles deep into Polly's rectum. Her reaction? She licked my face.

The vet, still probing, said, "Oh. Now you see, here we go. There should be a little more resistance or reaction to this." The ever-cute Polly actually looked over her shoulder and smiled at the vet.

I am thinking, "Thank you Captain Obvious. I'm no veterinarian, but even I know that it is unusual for a dog to have no reaction whatsoever to a three knuckler up the butt. What does it mean?" So, I asked, "What does it mean?"

He dropped the bomb. "My guess would be that she has a neurological disorder that has resulted in her having no feeling in her

133

elimination tracts. That would explain why the waste just falls out of her. She has no muscular function to control it."

"What can we do?"

"Not much."

"You mean we have to have her put down?"

"That would be my suggestion. The Dumb Friends League will take her off your hands. I'll write a note of explanation. Can you give me the name of the people who sold you this dog? It looks like a puppy mill." I had the information on the mom and son with me and gave it to him.

When I got home with Polly, I caught Julie first and we talked about what to do. We had called the lady and her son the night before with a question about the stream of eliminations coming from Polly and had an ugly confrontation with the son. He was a scary guy over the phone, and they had our address. My wife was home alone all day with our kids, so I filed our solution to this problem under "Make no big mistakes." I thought angering someone who looked like the messed-up guy in *The Goonies* over $600 fell into this category.

Julie asked me to let things go and not press it. "You gave the vet their names, and I don't want to be threatened over $600. Please can we let this go and chalk it up to a huge mistake? The son scares me. He was…"

I jumped in, "…exactly like the messed-up guy in *Goonies*, I know. He freaked me out too." She looked at me quizzically, missing the *Goonies* reference. I continued, "I agree we let this go. Going there in the first place was the big mistake, and I pushed for that. My bad. What are we going to do about a dog for Kelsey?"

Julie looked at me with her own puppy dog eyes that to this day can still control me. I realized I was about to be the proud owner of an $1,800 bulldog – Polly II, of Christmas letter fame. I called the ad in the paper, was assured that they had some puppies left for us to see the next night, and then I went to talk to the kids.

I explained, "Polly has no feeling in her bowels and cannot be an inside dog because she poops and pees everywhere – as we all know. I am going to take her to the Dumb Friends League tomorrow and they will find a home for her at a farm by a river, where it won't matter that poop and pee fall out of her. She will be really happy there as an outdoor dog. We are then going to get another bulldog puppy tomorrow night. So, we need to say goodbye to Polly tonight." The farm Polly I went to was sadly not real like the farm Cinnamon, our wild golden retriever, had gone to years earlier.

It was a tough night, softened by Polly II's arrival the following evening. The provider had written the necessary checks to make everything okay and I was, for a brief moment, a champion in my wife's eyes – a good dog. Life was sweet in the comfortable nest and I didn't care that I had bought myself in. For the next 6 years, Polly II would worship me every evening when I came home from work, the same way Ginger does to this day, in recognition of my role as the provider. One good dog always appreciates another.

HAPPY HOLIDAYS FROM THE HENDERSONS

November in Colorado was extraordinarily beautiful this year and the gorgeous fall weather provided the opportunity for me to get the outdoor Christmas lights done the day after Thanksgiving. I was thankful for this and feeling my oats about my efficiency until it became clear that what I had done wasn't cutting it for Julie. I knew this when she gently approached me two days after I had finished the decorations and said, "Thanks for putting up the Christmas decorations so efficiently this year. Um, just a thought, something I want you to mull over, but I have an idea to do something a little different this year." Since I speak fluent Julie after 26 years, I knew that this meant what I had done looked lousy, she hated it, and it was coming down.

We struggle by comparison in outdoor holiday decorations every year because we live across the street from a "Griswold" type home. They decorate every year for Halloween, Thanksgiving, and Christmas in a manner that can only be described as intimidating – millions of lights, sound effects, live animals, rides etc. We never have enough lights to compete, despite a $100 investment in new lights every year. My aesthetic mistake this year was that I found a couple of boxes full of "white corded" white icicle lights (for draping from the gutters) that I haven't used since I had a near death experience on the ladder a number of years ago. I thought, "There are thousands and thousands of white lights here that we haven't used for years. If I add these to what we have done the past few years our house will light up like the Star in the East long ago." I thus proceeded to drape the "white corded" white icicle lights over trees and bushes in an admittedly haphazard fashion while Julie was out shopping. I say "white corded" a lot because apparently this was a big mistake.

While at night the trees and bushes did indeed light up, during the day the house apparently looked stupid, like white dreadlocks had been indiscriminately tossed around our yard. Julie lived with this for two days and then said something. She took me outside and said, "I know that you leave for work in the dark and come home in the dark, so I thought you should take a real hard look at the house in the daylight with me. What do you think?" "Looks great," I replied (clueless).

She prodded, "Don't you think the white cords everywhere look kind of, um, stupid? I mean look at the other homes around us – we stick out this year."

I quickly calculated that any agreement on my part was going to result in us having to completely redo the outside decorations. So, I fought for my creative passion. "I think that trying to look like everyone else is not very creative. No other house on the block looks like this during the day – we clearly have decorated for Christmas and are not hiding that fact during the day with "green corded" lights like our neighbors are. With all the political fighting over retailers not recognizing Christmas, I thought that we should take a stand and show that we are celebrating Christmas in our yard day and night!" Hard as it may be to believe, this passionate argument fell on deaf ears and Julie and I spent two days taking down my "white corded" masterpiece and putting up new decorations. The house looks better, I guess.

I share all of this decorating stuff with our friends and family this year as an early cry for help. With Brett out of the house and working since January, Matthew graduating from CSU next December, and Kelsey going to college next August, I will soon be left alone with Julie. Clearly Julie's mothering instincts are not going to struggle to find a home as I was reprimanded for the equivalent of coloring outside the lines this year on Christmas decorations. The last time I was scrutinized this closely by Julie was when I was coaching the kids and getting tossed from games. So, while this annual letter brings sincere wishes for a Merry Christmas and a Happy New Year 2006 to all of our friends and family members, it also is a cry for help from our nearly empty nest: Please come visit us (and live with us if you want) to take some of the focus off me!

Love, Ted, Julie, Brett, Matthew and Kelsey

CHAPTER 9
SHOWING UP AS COACH

The last of the showing up triumvirate was actually a subset of showing up as dad because coaching was really all about being able to be with my kids in an environment where we could have fun, compete, and learn valuable life lessons together. I could easily tie sports into my broad lecture platform and coaching provided a great pulpit.

Coaching can be similar to raising kids—it's more fun when the children are younger. As the kids grow, other parents start to go crazy. Once certain parents started to believe (wrongly) that their child's youth sports experience would make or break their potential to play in high school, college, and professionally, coaching became less fun. The pressure on the coach was much less when 'equal play' was dictated and everyone understood that this was all about the kids and not the parents.

When the kids were old enough to start playing sports – unbelievably soccer and T-Ball started at 6 years old – I was ready to volunteer to coach them. I had enough of an athletic background to have confidence in my abilities to teach various team sports, and I had listened enough as a player to understand that coaches get to lecture. I knew that the team sports backdrop would provide ample opportunity for me to continue to drive home foundation points to my kids and my coaching charges. The youth sports programs were always looking for Dads that were willing to coach, and I was happy to volunteer.

In hindsight, I would've loved to have built a career as a coach, but the path never presented itself after I stumbled into business. Youth sports provided me the opportunity to fulfill this latent desire, and I coached roughly 35 teams in soccer, baseball, and basketball over a 12-year period during my children's formative years. I coached all three of my kids at various ages before high school and gained further confirmation that boys and girls are indeed different.

GIRLS BASKETBALL: 10-year-old Kelsey was dribbling the ball and had not yet crossed half court – no pressing in the back court at this point. I said, "Kelsey, run Play One." This was Play One of two that I was instructing her to run. Play One was designed to get the ball to Stephanie on the right wing. Play Two was designed to get the ball to Stephanie anyway you could. Stephanie was our horse and she would go on to be a Division 1 college athlete. Kelsey stopped dribbling, listened to me, nodded, and then proceeded to start dribbling again towards half court. The referee called her for double dribble.

She turned and looked at me and said, "Daddy that was your fault! You have to stop talking to me during the game! I can't dribble and listen to you at the same time!"

This did not turn out to be one of Kelsey's better games, and Stephanie saved the day for us at the end where we won at the buzzer. So, on the way home Kelsey was kind of quiet until I tried to say something complementary about our team and the close game we had just had. At this point my daughter gave me an earful, "I don't know what difference it makes. You yell, 'Run Play One, run Play Two' - it's stupid. Everything is to get the ball to Stephanie anyway. If she is so great, why don't you just adopt her?"

I looked at her in the rear-view mirror and asked, "Do you think she's available? I mean her parents seem to love her and stuff. Should I try?"

My 10-year-old daughter started to cry (pretty much a fake cry) and said, "You're mean Daddy..." then she took a below the belt shot that hurt..."and a bad coach!"

BOYS BASEBALL: One of the coaching challenges in 10-year-old baseball is to get the kids who are deathly afraid of the ball to stand in there and take a good cut. The problem is that many 10-year-old pitchers have little or no control and are likely to hit anybody at any time. So, we practiced turning away from an inside pitch saying, "If you are going to get hit, turn so you get hit in the back."

I had a kid, Daniel, who simply could not get the hang of this and was terrified of any inside pitched ball. In fairness to him, he had been dinged a few more times than the other kids so his fear was

140

understandable. When an inside pitch came, his tendency was to panic and open himself up to the pitch. This was dangerous, because some 10-year-olds, although they have no control, can bring it. During a game, I was coaching from third base and Daniel was hitting. An inside strike came and he all but ran out of the box. I yelled to him, "Daniel! He is not going to hit you. Stay in there and take a good rip. If the ball comes inside, turn away from it like we practiced. But you have to stay in there. You are looking good. This next one is going to be perfect for you. He is not going to hit you. Hang in there and take a good rip at it."

The next pitch was way inside, and he panicked and opened himself up as if surrendering. The pitch nailed him with a direct hit. He dropped his bat, grabbed his crotch and started screaming, "My dick! He hit me in the dick! Coach, you said he wouldn't hit me and he hit me in the dick!"

THE LESSON: Whether I was coaching girls or boys, no matter the sport, when something went wrong it was always my fault. I was okay with this. I had been married to Julie long enough to recognize the apparent fact that most everything that went wrong in life was my fault.

I was a 'life lessons through sports' kind of coach and I easily transitioned three of the four foundation lectures to the athletic fields. To be a part of any team, you had to show up and at the first practice of every season, I made a point of congratulating all my players on the fact that they were willing to do this and be a part of a team. I gave this lecture often throughout the season as an encouragement that showing up and making the effort to improve was what youth team sports was really all about. I promised that we would have a supportive environment where every kid would see a measurable arc of improvement in their skills if they we were willing to show up and try.

Once it was established that the team would be a loyal atmosphere where we were all going to show up and try to improve, the leap to rights and responsibilities was easy. "All 13 of you signed up to play and are showing up for practices twice a week. With the right to be on this team comes some responsibility that I want to address. You have the responsibility to work on your own personal arc of improvement so that you can contribute to the efforts to make our *team* better throughout this season. You have a responsibility to show your coaches and your teammates respect. You have a responsibility to be a positive part of this team whether you are in the field or on the bench. Put the team ahead of yourself."

I often taught that if you could figure out how to take responsibility and be a contributing part of a team environment as a young kid, it would help you as an adult. You would be able to understand what it meant to contribute to a diverse workforce within a company when you eventually went to work. Youth sports was a great training ground for kids to learn at an early age that everyone had a role to play and not everyone batted cleanup.

I also pointed out that the coach had a responsibility to determine who would start, who would sit on the bench, and where the kids would play, and that the coach was not infallible in making these decisions. "You don't get to choose your coach anymore than you get to choose your teachers or your boss later in life. Some are better than others and you have to deal with it and get through the season. Sometimes you will find yourself on the bench when you don't think it is fair. You can handle this one of two ways – you can pout and hang your head, or you can hold your head up high and contribute to this team and try your best to prove your coach wrong. Life isn't always fair and you might as well learn that right now. You can't quit because you don't think the coach is being fair to you. You have the responsibility to hang in there and finish the season and do your best to improve and contribute to the team overall."

I was blessed with good kids throughout my coaching tenure and since complaining and pouting from the kids always began with a parent lighting the flame at home, I was thankful that most of my charges, parents seemed to be supportive of my bigger picture efforts even if they felt their child was being stiffed. In other words, I was blessed to have a limited number of crazy parents in my 12-year coaching career.

The third foundation lecture found a home in my coaching platform because it was easy to identify sports as play, a healthy part of a balanced life. Choice was involved in being a part of a team. The balanced life lecture was usually given sometime after a mid-late season practice. "We have built a pretty good team this year and I am very proud of you guys and the effort you have all made to make us better. Once in a while, because we take things seriously out here and we are playing to win, I want to remind you to keep sports and this season in perspective. I want to make sure that you understand that all this sports stuff is only a small part of your life."

I continued, "If playing sports means everything to you, way above all else, then your life is lacking balance. If something goes wrong for you in sports, all the eggs in your one basket break and you become pretty unhappy. So, don't take this sports stuff too seriously, it is just a small part of your life. We will work hard and try to be the best we can be, but at the end of the day, we all go home to other things in our lives — family, friends, school, work, church, etc. You all have a heck of a lot more going on in your life than just this team or just this season."

I usually only gave this lecture a couple of times a year as a big picture talk. I never gave it after games. Never, that is, until we met up with the Colorado Reds baseball organization. The Reds were the Colorado youth baseball equivalent of the Evil Empire. The Reds were the team that was formed by a coach who simply outworked all the other volunteer coaches. He scouted players and opposing teams with a passion and upgraded his team every year. They played in out of state tournaments all the time and logged over 80 games a summer.

In a year when our team lost only 8 games out of over 70, 5 of those losses were to the Reds. We never beat them, and we were a pretty good team. They were just better than everybody else, and they knew it. One of the Reds parents said to me before we were about to play them one weekday summer evening, "We are ranked sixth in the country."

I stumbled a bit at this disclosure and was dying to ask where the 12-year-old national baseball rankings were published. This seemed a complete absurdity to me, but this dad was dead serious — the Reds were the sixth best 12-year-old team in the United States of America.

He continued on about a tournament they had just returned from in California, "We took second last weekend in a monster tournament near L.A. It was awesome and we played unbelievably well. Some pro scouts came out to watch us play. Dodgers and Angels scouts. That was pretty exciting for the kids."

Unsure how to respond, I said, "Wow. And here you are back in Colorado on a Wednesday night to kick the shit out of us again. This has to be a let down for you guys."

Deep breath and dead serious, "Yeah, it really is."

The Reds then proceeded to kick the shit out of us again. My kids were pretty down after the game and I was looking to lift them up a bit. The balanced life lecture was about all I had to offer. "I am proud of you guys as always. You played hard until the last out – which unfortunately came early when we got 10-runned in the fifth inning by these guys again. I'm not going to lie to you all - I hate the Reds. I hate their coaches, their players and their parents." I paused here and realized I had to back off a bit as the kids might not see the tongue in cheek part of this post game speech.

"Okay, that is a bit harsh. Nothing in little league baseball should cause us to hate someone, and I don't. We all know a lot of parents and players on the Reds and they are good people. Their team name is totally appropriate because they are essentially all Communists, but good comrades. Unfortunately, I think that after nine straight losses to them, it is time to acknowledge that they are simply a better team than we are. There is no shame in that, and I have to take most of the blame - the fact is that their coach simply out works your coach. I actually heard he was at the hospital last week looking at some of the new born babies for future Reds prospects. These guys take their little league baseball very seriously. They practice all year round, they play more games against better competition than we do, they scout every team in the western hemisphere, and they use performance enhancing drugs – okay, not really."

I was getting some smiles, so I pressed on. "They have the best uniforms and the best warm-up jackets. They have the best bat bags, personalized in gold trim. When they travel, they fly first class and hit on the stewardesses the whole flight. They recruit nationally and even have inroads to some Cuban players seeking to escape the Castro regime. Each player on the Reds has a personal masseuse and a year-round tutor to help keep them eligible – whatever that means at age 12. It is just tough for us to compete with that and maintain proper balance in out lives." This was where I delivered the balanced life lecture in a quick and disciplined manner, pointing out that in our well-balanced lives, the losses to the Reds didn't really matter that much.

I then turned to the positive, "That said, I have it on good authority that the Reds are ranked sixth in the nation for 12-year-old baseball teams. Let's take their ranking and do some math. Okay? I mean 5 of our 8 losses this year are to the Reds, the sixth best team in the country. We are like 64 and 8, right?" I got an affirmation from Mike Lindquist, my long-suffering assistant coach.

I continued, "If they are sixth in the country for 12-year-olds, I figure we have to be at least in the top 20 nationally, right? So, let's go with that on our resumes and feel good about ourselves."

I went into the Saturday Night Live Jon Lovitz liar guy impression: "Yeah, that's the ticket. You guys play for a team that is ranked in the top 20 in the nation. In fact, yeah, that's right - we are the 17th best 12-year-old team in the United States of America. Yeah, that's right. 17th in the whole country. That's the ticket!"

Back to myself, "So hold your heads up. We have beaten everyone else in the state but the Reds this year. You have worked very hard to accomplish that. We have a very good team and I am very proud of all you guys - I won't let the Evil Empire Reds ruin that fact for us. So, go home and hug your Moms, who—by the way—are much better looking than the Reds Moms, and enjoy the rest of your week. I'll see you at practice Friday afternoon."

I would always throw a compliment out to our Moms after the Reds had hammered us. After these (not very close) losses to the Reds, my players needed their Moms and the kind of love only they could provide. My wife even took pity on me after a loss to the Reds and I was rarely in trouble with her after they had shellacked us because the games were often not close. If the games weren't close, I rarely got into too much trouble with the umpires. It was umpires and referees that most frequently triggered my temper and got me into trouble in my marriage.

At this point, it probably seems like I was a reasonable influence for the kids that I coached. However, it must be pointed out that some of my character flaws (temper) most prominently emerged when I was coaching, especially during games. I can say with confidence that I was absolutely a model coach when it came to practices. We worked hard on fundamentals, focused on each individual player's arc of improvement, and taught foundation type lessons while using the team sport as a backdrop.

Unfortunately, in addition to practices, we also had to play games. For the most part I truly believe that the parents and players of the 35-plus teams that I coached would say the overall experience with me was very positive, from many perspectives. My wife even acknowledges that I was a good coach, even though I was somewhat of an embarrassment to her at times.

You see, I was the coach that gets thrown out of games once in a while. I was the coach who was extremely loud, always encouraging to my kids, but very loud when it came to the officials. I have been thrown out of games while coaching all three of my children – probably about 10 times in all over a twelve-year stretch. Lead by example? I spent many hours lecturing my kids about what NOT to do using myself as the primary example. Coaching was the arena where I was most likely to ask my children to "Do as I say and not as I do," an admittedly pathetic request from a responsible Dad.

In a particularly bad moment, I was thrown out of an 11-year-old girl's basketball game and caused my daughter to cry. Her brothers were in the stands, stunned that their Dad could get so fired up about 11-year-old girls' basketball. Team Mom Julie was running the scoreboard, thoroughly humiliated, thinking "Yeah, that's my old man" as I was escorted out of the gym. I had thrown my clipboard across the floor because a referee had made a series of bad calls – no excuse other than I lost it and tossed it. YIKES! I made my apologies to my players and their parents after the game in the parking lot because I had been banished from the gym. I confirmed practice on Monday night and took the long walk to the car with my entire family.

Kelsey immediately took my side, "I told the ref that you were my Dad and he shouldn't have thrown you out."

I threw my arm around her and said, "Well the truth is I should have been thrown out for what I did. My temper got the best of me. I was wrong, and I deserved the consequences of my actions. I was way out of line."

16-year-old Brett said, "Dad. That was awesome. I mean, you got thrown out of a girl's basketball game – and you were up by six! Dude, you are way too fired up about this."

14-year-old Matthew chimed in laughing, "It was *totally* awesome. You go to the ref, 'It slipped'. I mean, you just threw your clipboard across the entire gym. The ref tosses you and you go, 'It slipped', all innocent-like. Classic. Dad, that was so funny."

Mom finally opined quite sarcastically, "Yeah that was a laugh riot. I know I enjoyed it."

I knew that there was an unofficial restraining order in place for me with Julie at this point. When I pulled something like this, again not very often, it was days before I could even attempt to approach her. The comfortable nest was decidedly uncomfortable for me after a performance like this. The car ride home was awful, dominated by a painful silence.

When we got home, I sat all three kids down and did my best to explain myself, "I am sorry for the way I acted tonight. I have struggled with my temper my whole life, and it has caused me some problems. I am old enough to know better, and should be able to control it, but sometimes I don't. I am not perfect. You guys know that because this is not the first time I have screwed up. It probably won't be the last."

I always started making amends with the kids first after an event like this because Mom was less likely to move on and invite me back into the comfortable nest than the kids were. "I will keep showing up and trying to do better, though, and I would hope that that fact earns your respect as you grow older. Dad is trying to be a good Dad, and I want to set a good example, but sometimes I won't, like tonight. I want the best for you, so I will use myself as an example of what not to do if I have screwed up. Tonight was one of those nights. I'm sorry."

I paused and then said under my breath, "Your Mom not talking to me the whole way home was pretty comfortable, wasn't it? I mean, I asked her like three things and she completely ignored me. Think I'm in any trouble? Consequences for my actions, kids - that's what this is all about. I'm in huge trouble with Mom here. Any help you can give me to get her to acknowledge my existence again will be appreciated." The kids smiled at me, and that meant I was starting the recovery process within the nest. Eventually Julie would come around.

I have to say that Julie was truly a stalwart supporter of me as a coach, even though I embarrassed her every once in a while. There is an anchor metaphor in there somewhere that I don't deserve. I never humiliated Julie by being too tough on my kids, I mortified her because I didn't get along very well with umpires and referees and accordingly got tossed from games once in a while. I sadly must admit that I was a complete jerk at times to officials and while this was always embarrassing, it was never enough to get me to completely stop my harangues. Officials easily got under my skin because they controlled the game and I couldn't do anything about it. Parents and other coaches I got along with fine, but the officials I struggled with.

There was only one coach who ever got me to the point of anger that I sometimes reached with officials. We were playing for the conference championship in a coach-pitch league when Matthew was about eight years old. We had arrived at the field (where we had never played before) 90 minutes ahead of game time, hoping to take batting practice as well as some grounders to get a feel for the infield. The other team was already on the field taking batting practice.

I went over to the opposing coach and introduced myself in a very friendly manner. The guy was watching his team hit and he barely even looked at me when I introduced myself. I said, "We are looking forward to a good game today, coach. This should be fun."

I dealt with the uncomfortable fact that he didn't shake my hand and replied, "Yeah. Whatever." He never took his eyes off his players on the field.

I pressed on. "Hey, can we get the infield in about an hour? We are just going to hit some in the outfield until then. Can you holler when you are done?"

Coldly he replied, "We got here first, and I don't have to let you have anything. You can take infield before the game when the umpire says so. We are going to hold the infield until then. We got here first."

I was stunned and taken aback. I hadn't had any experience like this before with any other coach. I stammered, "Whatever works for you coach," and walked away doing a slow burn.

Game time was starting to approach, and we still hadn't had a chance at the infield. I was glaring at the opposing coach from the outfield. I recognized one of the umpires who had just arrived, a 20-something young man that had umped some of our earlier games, and I ran over to him. "Hey, ump. How are you doing today?" He returned the pleasantry, and I continued while handing him our lineup card, "Here is our lineup. Can we get some infield in before the game?"

He said, "For playoff games, there is no infield. We are going to drag the field and re-line it right now, and game time is in 10 minutes. No one is allowed on the infield after we drag it."

The opposing coach had come to within earshot now and heard my request. He interrupted and said, "Hey Ump, how are you doing? No infield before playoff games, right? We'll get off so you can drag it." He then met my eyes and smiled at me.

The ump greeted the opposing coach, "Hey coach. Yeah, that's right. We drag it and then start. Let's do the coin flip right now since you are both here, okay?"

I was going crazy, and wanted to throttle this coach who, although he didn't know it, was pushing my buttons as effectively as my brother could. After the coin flip, which I lost, it came time to shake hands, and I couldn't stand it any longer. I gripped his hand as hard as I could and when he started to pull away, I pulled him in close and looked him straight in the eyes and quietly said, "I've been watching your kids warm up. I just want you to know ahead of time that we are going to beat you like a **** drum today, okay coach?"

He looked at me a bit startled, and the umpire stepped in and said, "C'mon guys, let's get going here."

I squeezed his hand again, "You are gonna get beat like a **** drum. My kids are going to destroy you today. I want you to enjoy it." I dropped his hand and jogged back to the dugout calling my charges in.

Long story short, we beat this guy's team like a **** drum. And it was great. To this day, the line up to shake hands afterwards remains one of my favorites. This guy was seething and didn't want to see me with a smile on my face offering a handshake. Once we shook hands, I held on so he could hear what I had to say. In a sympathetic tone I said to him, "Wow coach, I am surprised. Honestly, we expected more of a game from you guys given all the extra infield your guys took. Good season, though."

Through clenched teeth and under his breath he responded, "**** you, ****."

I point out that no one at the game had any idea about our little confrontation. Sometimes it was the game behind the game that I enjoyed the most, watching a coach who took things way too seriously twist in the wind after we had hammered them. I'm sure the Reds coach enjoyed watching me twist also, and I did every time they beat us.

Despite the craziness, which I admit I contributed to, I enjoyed my years coaching youth sports. The whole experience was positive for me and the kids and lessons were learned by both of us. This was play in the balanced life and once the choice was made to participate as a player and a coach, rights and responsibilities were triggered. The kids learned about team over individual and the team concept stuff was extrapolated to the real world of the workplace they would eventually be a part of.

I viewed the teams I coached as mini-families and I tried to develop a reasonably comfortable nest every season where my players could improve, learn, socialize, and have some fun. It was ultimately encouraging to see so many fine young boys and girls competing in youth sports. I knew that for every kid I saw at the athletic field there were dozens more somewhere else playing an instrument, painting, singing, writing, or dancing – all being productive and improving themselves. When I coached, I often looked at the populated athletic fields in my God Bless America mode, made the obvious extrapolation, and felt good about the future of the country my grandchildren will call home.

I remember standing with my Dad at a ball field one summer day after a game I was coaching had ended. He was visiting from Chicago, was in his seventies, and was looking absently at the many games that were going on in the complex around him with a big grin on his face. I had finished my post game talk and I walked up to him and put my arm around his shoulder and said, "Hey Pops, ready to go?"

He turned to me and said, "This is great. All these kids are already participating. Look at this. They will develop a good work ethic and sports will provide a good platform for them to learn to survive and flourish in a competitive environment. They will all eventually have to house and feed themselves - two great motivators, good for the economic future of the country. Isn't youth sports great?" I just nodded and gave him a hug.

DECEMBER 2006

HAPPY HOLIDAYS FROM THE HENDERSONS

It is late November and I find myself in the unusual position of not struggling to come up with something to write about in our annual Christmas letter and my challenge is to communicate everything in a single page. Therefore, I will eliminate the mindless banter that usually defines our first paragraph and get to the important stuff.

Despite what my Dad and Julie thought for most of 2006, I have not completely lost my mind. I will, however, admit that I am in the throes of a significant mid-life crisis that was triggered by the prospect of Kelsey leaving for college in August. So what kind of mid-life craziness did I come up with?

For starters, I quit my job as an analyst in May, eliminating the stress, pressure, and horrible hours of my Wall Street existence, along with eliminating my earning potential. Dad and Julie both asked the logical question, "So, what are you going to do after you quit?" This is where things got a bit dicey because I told them that my plan was to write a book. They both agreed that this was not a plan but more of a dream, and shouldn't I keep my job while I pursued a dream? The answer from me was a truculent, "No. I should quit the job I hate and write my book." So, I did. Sticking with Christmas letter tradition, Julie plays the villain to my hero in the book, so you know it is a true story.

That is all I will say about the book because Julie is absolutely sick of hearing about it - and I don't understand why. Anyway, she has been dealing with her own issues in adjusting to the empty nest. She is living alone with me and Ginger now, and the bulldog is old and sleeps all the time. Since I am not working, I have picked up Ginger's habit of following Julie around the house, and I frequently ask her if she will play with me or if there is anything I can do to help her. I interpret responses like "Please, just go away," to mean that I should come back later. I have found out it really means go away...and stay there. I keep forgetting that she has a life without me – how sad that must be for her. We celebrated 27 years together in October.

Brett (24) has been living and working in Denver for the past two years and is enjoying adult single life. Trips to Las Vegas are commonplace as are flag football and softball leagues. Golf with Dad is not only tolerated but enjoyed. Brett recently recognized that he is about the same age as I was when he was born. He quickly commented that he was not ready to be a Dad. Since he doesn't have a steady girlfriend, I took this as great news.

Matthew (22) will graduate from Colorado State this December and start working for Protiviti in Denver in January. I don't know how excited Matthew is to be an accountant because he always plays his cards close to the vest. I have tried to be encouraging, reminding him that although I started in accounting, I had a career that went in a lot of different directions. To which he responded, "Yeah Dad. You had a great Wall Street job. Now you are writing a book? What a meltdown. I promise that I won't lose it like you have." (Editor's note: Anyone who knows me is aware that this is not how I talk. These are Dad's own true feelings about his decision. He is just trying to pin them on me. - Matt). Unfortunately, true.

Kelsey (19) unbelievably left for college in August. She is a freshman at the University of Northern Colorado and is majoring in psychology. Julie and I are already feeling sorry for whomever Kelsey eventually marries because she argues like I do. Kelsey believes that louder and more aggressive often wins and when she combines that attitude with some psychological training, look out, she is going to be tough to argue with. But hey, isn't that what a good marriage is all about anyway?

On a serious note, Kelsey is in dialogue with the Mayo Clinic and is likely to take steps towards seeing if she is a possible surgery candidate for her epilepsy next summer. This has been a lengthy journey and although surgery is a long shot, it is the only way to completely cure her seizures and Kelsey wants to pursue this. We are hopeful for her.

On a somber note, many of you know that my Dad passed away unexpectedly at the age of 82 in October. We have done everything possible to celebrate a life that was lived to the fullest by a man who would have no regrets about the way he lived or died. We miss him greatly and are reminded at this time of year how blessed we were to have Dad in our lives.

We Wish You the Merriest of Christmases and a New Year 2007
Full of Joy!

LOVE, TED, JULIE, BRETT, MATTHEW AND KELSEY

CHAPTER 10
BUMPS IN THE ROAD

If there was an eleventh lecture, this was it. It was the theme that ran through all of Dad's sermons and it was focused in the reality of his childhood during the Great Depression. Dad's view of the world often went to a worst-case scenario and then calibrated backwards. He made it clear in most every talk he gave that following the basics was not a recipe for guaranteed happiness. If we were lucky enough to live long, happy, independent, and productive lives, it was inevitable that we would encounter some severe bumps in the road of life. "Life is not easy and you are going to take some hits."

'Bumps in the road' was his short-hand term for the inevitable drama, trauma, and tragedy that everyone encounters in life. He preached, "Such is life. You can choose to let the bumps define you, or you can recognize the simple fact that everyone – and I mean everyone - is dealing with something and that even with all the dips life is basically good. Live it to the fullest and enjoy your short time here. That is what fighting the good fight means."

He and Mom made the same point in different ways. Dad, harkening back to the way he delivered the 'show up' lecture, sometimes delivered the bumps in the road theme in an aggressive way, "People don't want to hear about your problems. They have their own problems to deal with. So quit bitching about the drama and trauma in your life and show up and deal with the adversity. Everyone is dealing with something, so don't over play your situation. I promise you that someone has it much worse than you do. If your life has balance, you can ride it out, whatever it is."

Mom, on the other hand, made the same point more compassionately, "You need to give people the benefit of the doubt, because you never know what they may be dealing with. If you run into someone who is surly or even down right mean, consider the fact that they may be dealing with something very serious, even tragic in their life. Don't judge people based on a single brief encounter, they may be struggling with something in their life that you can't even imagine. Someone may have just lost their child. Stuff happens all the time, just keep your eyes open as you get older and make sure to have compassion for others. Everybody is dealing with something." Mom and Dad in lock step delivery from completely different perspectives. Gotta love consistent parenting.

My Dad was afraid that my idea to quit my job to write a book was a self-inflicted bump in the road and he did not hide his concern from me. He tried to get me to see reason before I officially quit saying "Who isn't burnt out on their job at age 50? You don't just walk away, you hang in there. You keep showing up, keep providing the income for the family. I don't understand why you are doing this. Writing a book? I don't get it. You have a good job that pays the bills. Are you crazy?"

Beyond Dad's frustration with me on the fundamental issue of quitting my job (work in the balanced life), another problem looming ahead was that he would eventually read the book. This was a bit of a problem, because I was worried about how conservative Dad, at 82 years old, would react to reading the passages on sex, masturbation, vasectomies, teenage drinking, and my other questionable musings. I was going to have to prepare him before he read anything, and my plan was to give Dad and Mom a first draft copy of the book for Christmas 2006. The problem was that I didn't have a chapter to end the book, something that would tie it together. A bump in the road triggered this ending chapter.

On October 9, 2006 my Dad died unexpectedly after what was to be a routine cardiac procedure. Everything stopped and moved in slow motion for a few weeks. While I am hurting, I am inspired by his passing because he lived a life that was inspirational in its simplicity. This book was written as a tribute to my Dad, a man who loved and worried about his three kids and found the lecture to be the vehicle that allowed him to reach them and teach them. Writing this last chapter just two months after he has passed allows me to pay full compliment to him without worrying that it would make him uncomfortable.

Interestingly, even though I haven't been a child for over 30 years, most of the memories that are hitting me are of my childhood: Dad lecturing me in his disciplined, but loving way; Dad teaching me how to swim, fish, ride a bike, throw, hit, catch, shoot, dribble, body surf, drive a car, and play golf; Dad marching through the house singing "*Seventy Six Trombones*" and getting us to follow him climbing over sofas and chairs and up and down the stairs.

More, Indian Guides campouts; his presence at every one of my youth league games; taking the family to church; Bears games at Wrigley and then Soldiers Field; Cubs games at Wrigley; Bulls games at the Stadium; rebounding for me in the driveway; helping me with homework; picking out a Christmas tree with the family; Christmas mornings; playing golf in father/son tournaments; crying and holding me tight when his Mom died; watching me play basketball in high school and talking to me excitedly after the games; seeing the pride in his eyes when I signed my scholarship to Auburn; the way he would say "This is the berries!" and remind me to stop and smell the roses. And the way he showed his love and affection for his family openly and unconditionally for over 50 years. These memories won't stop, and I don't want them to. But the result is that, at almost 50 years old, I miss my Daddy.

My memories aren't exclusively of my youth, as I also miss the Dad I loved as an adult. He remained a constant throughout my life and was a common-sense sounding board for virtually every important decision that I made as I navigated life independently. I was in awe of the wonderful life he and Mom had built that remained centered around their faith, their three kids, their ten grandchildren and their wonderful friends. Despite the fact that we lived hundreds of miles from each other for over 25 years, I know that nothing was left unsaid between Dad and I and that knowledge has helped get me through this tough time.

When I say nothing was left unsaid, that includes him telling me for most of this year that he thought I was crazy for quitting a good job and trying to write a book. His frustrated refrain was, "Why don't you keep doing your job *and* write the book? I don't understand why you need to quit your job."

I told him exactly why, "Dad, I hate my job and it is negatively impacting my life at home and everywhere else. The job works because of the money, but that is the only reason it works – I hate it. If I don't quit and force a change in my life now, I know I never will.

As I approach 50, I want to chronicle something for the kids and grandkids that will mean something to them. I am energized by the fact that I actually have the nerve to quit my job and do this, knowing that everyone thinks I'm crazy, knowing that I may fail spectacularly and look like an idiot – but being happy with the guy in the mirror. I am enjoying this. Based on the way you raised me, you of all people should be able to relate." He smiled at this but was still worried.

As 2006 wore on and I officially quit my job, Dad gave up the ghost on talking me out of my work decision and showed his first real interest in the book saying, "So, tell me some more about the book. Beyond your mid-life crisis, what is it going to be about?"

I said, "It is basically going to be a book documenting my efforts to not screw up the kids. The underlying theme is a tribute to the millions of fathers who are showing up and making an effort to be a good Dad every day – flaws and all, just like you did. I'm going to title it *"Dad's Top Ten Lectures"* and at its core are the lectures that you gave to Bart, Holly, and me when we were growing up." I paused and looked at him sincerely, "You're my hero Pop. Always have been."

I could see that he was uncomfortable with the notion that the book might come off as a kind of tribute to him, and he reacted with concern. "Ted, please don't tell me you are going to make it sound like I was this great Dad or anything. You know I am a flawed man. Mom and I were very lucky to have three children who were receptive to a common-sense message and understood the unconditional love thing. We were blessed with wonderful kids who communicated with us. Don't try to make me look better than I was."

I found this interesting. This was exactly the same reaction Julie had when I told her I was going to write the book. She said to me, "Don't make us look better as parents than we really were. We were lucky and blessed with good kids." Imagine that. This was probably the third time Julie and my Dad were in lock step agreement on anything in over 27 years. They both didn't want me to make them look better than they really were as parents and they both felt that they were lucky to have good kids, nothing more. I reminded them of something Dad had said to me when I was growing up, "Luck can definitely come into play in life, but never forget that those who consistently show up tend to be a lot luckier than those that don't."

What I remember most was Dad getting over his worry (never easy) and telling me how happy he was that I was doing something I was passionate about. He would say, "You sound great. I can tell you are enjoying writing your book - I can hear it in your voice every time we talk. I am happy for you. Whether it works out or not, I am proud of you for taking this shot." He was my Dad, I was his son - he still knew exactly what to say to me at 82 years of age. He later told me that he was looking forward to reading the book at Christmas when I was done with the first draft. Unfortunately, he never got to read a single page. I imagine Dad is sitting up in heaven looking down at me and saying, "There, Ted. I gave you an ending to your book. Now finish it and quit talking to everybody about it. Then get a real job that pays the bills."

I remember as my family gathered at Dad's funeral that I mentioned how upset and vocal Dad was about me quitting my job to write a book. My Mom quickly jumped in and said, "Ted, he was never upset with you. You know Dad. He was worried. That's all. Quitting your job at age 50 without a net made him worry for you. He was so proud of you."

My older brother Bart piped in, "Yeah Mom. But you've got to admit that it sounds like the book thing is probably what killed Dad. I think it's safe to say its Ted's fault Dad is gone." We all shared a gallows' laugh that my Dad would have definitely enjoyed.

This chapter is not only a tribute to my Dad, but to the other person in my life that I was proud to call Dad, my father-in-law, Ron Pinchback. The first bump in our family's road was when Julie's Dad passed away unexpectedly at the age of 61 in January 1993. I regret that I only had 14 years with him as my Dad since there was much I could have learned from him, how not to worry so much topping the list. Like my Dad, he loved his life and lived it to the fullest. His life remained centered around his faith, his family, and his friends until the day he died. If Julie and I had screwed up as parents after having the examples that both our parents set for us, we should have been shot.

My Dad recently repeated something he had been saying for a while, "You know how I have always said that life is a long race, not a sprint?" I nodded. "The interesting paradox is that it is a long race that is over in the blink of an eye. So, if I go tomorrow, I want you to know that I have no regrets. I love my life and I feel like I have left nothing on the table in terms of the way I have lived it. If I go tomorrow, celebrate!"

I have no doubt that this was Dad Pinchback's attitude about his life when he passed also, and although my children hate to hear me say it, I feel exactly the same way at this point in my life. If I go tomorrow, I will have absolutely no regrets and I would want people to celebrate how much I have enjoyed my life, not grieve about my passing.

October 9, 2006 turned out to be tomorrow for my Dad, and we have done everything in our power to celebrate the life that he lived and loved, acknowledge and deal with this inevitable bump, and move forward positively, taking care of Mom as Dad would expect. There is no question that Mom will fare much better without Dad than vice versa, so there is a sense of order in Mom surviving Dad. We all knew that Dad readily admitted that nothing in his life worked without Mom and that she was the glue that held our family, and his life, together.

Dad died knowing that his life was in order and that he had been a good husband and a good father, because he got the only votes that mattered. He and Mom had raised an outwardly affectionate set of children, and my brother, sister, and I always let Dad and Mom know that we loved them and appreciated everything they had done for us.

As for my own efforts as a Dad over the past 25 years, they have not gone unrewarded. The outpouring of love and affection from my children as they stood by my side in Chicago in October to say goodbye to their only remaining Grandpa, was overwhelming to me. I know that my children loved their Grandfather and will miss him, but what I saw in their eyes was the unconditional love and concern that they had for me because I was hurting so much and often falling apart emotionally.

Like my own Dad, I already know that I have been a good father because I've gotten the only votes that matter. We too have raised an outwardly affectionate set of children and my kids have never been hesitant in letting Julie and I know they love us and appreciate the effort we have made as parents. They have lived long enough to recognize that every family doesn't operate the way we do, yet they have been accepting and embracing of our crazy notion of how to live a happy, productive, and fulfilling life. When Dad Pinchback died, the kids were too young to understand the outpouring of love and affection from hundreds of friends and family members that marked the end of a life well lived. With my Dad, they were old enough to understand the tribute that was paid to the man.

I still love being a Dad and know that I am not done yet — never will be if I follow my own Dad's example. The best part is that when I look into my children's eyes, I can still see the babies that they were as well as the adults they have become, and I am reminded of the wonderful parent/child journey we have taken together. I am overwhelmed by the love I feel for them and that passion still causes me to worry. No matter. I have come to grips with the fact that I worry, and I still consider being a Dad to be the absolute coolest thing in the world. I think I'm ready for grandkids.

HAPPY HOLIDAYS FROM THE HENDERSONS

I begin this letter on a serious note in recognition of the fact that 2007 has been a very special year for our family. In July we celebrated what was for us, a miracle, as Kelsey endured two brain surgeries at the Mayo Clinic in an attempt to rid her life of epileptic seizures. This has been a lifelong struggle for Kelsey and as 2007 comes to an end we are thrilled to report that she has not had a seizure in over 5 months – the longest seizure free period in her life. We remain in a state of constant celebration and praise.

As people of faith, we recognize that there is no greater gift a friend or family member can offer than to pray for you. We were touched by how many of you hit your knees for Kelsey and will never forget the love and support that we felt (and needed) while at Mayo this summer. This annual correspondence is an inadequate forum to express our true appreciation, but we want to thank you all very much for your compassion, kindness, and prayers.

As the family's primary worrier, I was thrilled to discover that the neurosurgeon didn't remove the part of Kelsey's brain that controls sense of humor and timing. Immediately after her second surgery while she was still in intensive care and a bit drugged, Kelsey slurred to me, "Daddy, I'm getting a puppy out of this." Um, yeah you are. New puppy Cubby (a puggle) joined our family in August and old bulldog Ginger is cranky about the disruption this has caused in her life. Ginger can't wait for Cubby to join Kelsey and her roommates next semester at Colorado State University. Julie and I are ready for Cubby to be in college also. We forgot how much work puppies are.

You might remember that last year I indulged my mid-life crisis, quit my job and wrote a book, successfully throwing our home into further turmoil and uncertainty during 2006 and 2007. After 28 years together, the last one in very close proximity to each other, Julie has just about had it with me and my "Life is an unplanned adventure" attitude. I am happy to report that my mid-life crisis has officially ended as I took a corporate development job with Dish Network in October, returning to my roots in multi-channel television, this time on the satellite side. See honey, everything turned out fine. And we have a book for the great grandchildren to read. So, this was really nothing more than a fun adventure.

THIS IS JULIE INSERTING A COMMENT: TED MAKES THE LAST TWO YEARS SOUND LIKE FUN, "LIFE IS AN UNPLANNED ADVENTURE". FUN IS NOT THE WORD I WOULD USE TO DESCRIBE THE LAST TWO YEARS IN OUR HOME. TED STARTED WORRYING ABOUT A WEEK AFTER HE QUIT HIS JOB – ABOUT EVERYTHING. WITH THAT MINDSET, HE WAS HOME ALL THE TIME WRITING HIS BOOK AND INTERUPTING MY LIFE. I LOVE HIM, BUT REALLY, NOT SO MUCH FUN.

How many times do I have to say it, Julie just isn't very funny. Anyway, I am confident that you can connect the dots on her changed life: Kelsey appears to be seizure free and I am working again. Euphoric is the only word that adequately describes her state of mind right now. With a healthy Kelsey at college and me working again there is a sense of normalcy that has returned to our home for the first time in quite a while. Bonus - Julie seems to like me better now.

Brett and Matthew reside close to each other in downtown Denver and are both working for a living. I can't update you too much on their lives because they are busy working and playing without me, but I can guess: Single life in Denver; Within walking distance of Coors Field and the exciting 2007 Colorado Rockies; With a job; With lots of friends; With plenty to do; Without a puppy (sorry Cubby); Without a worry. Yeah, the boys are doing fine. I remember when I didn't worry...a long time ago in a galaxy...

In closing, we want to thank everyone again for their thoughts and prayers this year. Family and friends make the journey bearable no matter where the sometimes-bumpy road takes you. We love you all. We wish you a very Merry Christmas and a 2008 filled with joy!

Love, Ted, Julie, Brett, Matthew and Kelsey

Finally, I want to acknowledge that while we were at Mayo this summer with Kelsey, I was also cured of something. After her first surgery, Kelsey was in intensive care for six straight days and had 24-hour care. You know what that means? Yep, nurses around the clock. I was initially freaked out a bit remembering my delivery room and vasectomy experiences from over 20 years ago, but I soon came to realize that this situation was totally different. I was no longer the idiot husband who had impregnated his wife and didn't have a clue what being a father was all about. Nurses hate that guy. I was now the concerned Daddy who was there for his 19-year-old baby girl. Nurses love that guy. After the way they cared for Kelsey in intensive care, I realized that I love them too.

HAPPY HOLIDAYS FROM THE HENDERSONS

I have been looking forward to 2008 for well over a decade because this was the year when Kelsey turned 21, a birthday that many parents find to be a relief. All three of our children have now passed this adult barrier, a parenting finish line of sorts that begs the question: "Why am I still writing this letter every year?" Adult children – yeah, this was the time of life where I envisioned Julie and I gazing into each other's eyes and falling in love all over again in a high school type fantasy. You remember how it was in high school. When the parents were gone and the teenage couple found themselves home all alone - and they were very interested in each other? That is exactly what my empty nest fantasy was: the kids are gone Julie and I find ourselves all alone – and she constantly wants to make out with me. COMMENT FROM JULIE: UMMM, THAT WAS NOT MY FANTASY. Anyway, in 2008 the empty nest was not yet meant to be.

This turned out to be a year where we welcomed Brett (26) back home with us as he went to broadcasting school to change his career path. The deal was for him to do dishes and clean the basement in lieu of cash rent payments. Let's just say it is a good thing I write the Christmas letter, so you don't have to hear Julie's opinion on how the rent played out. Forever the optimist, Julie has packed cleaning stuff for our now departing oldest son. We are saying our goodbyes to Brett as he has accepted a job at a radio station in Winner, South Dakota starting at the end of December.

I think Matthew (24) will miss Brett most of all because he was his reliable companion for those infrequent weekend trips to Las Vegas. While Matthew will miss Brett, he will continue to journey to Vegas without him. As much as Matthew enjoys his older brother's company, comparatively Winner is a loser. Matthew and Brett got a bonus farewell trip with the family to Sin City in August for Kelsey's big day as she passed the official adult mark.

Now that Kelsey (a junior at Colorado State majoring in Human Development and Family Studies) has passed the mark, Julie only has me left to go. She recently confirmed in one of Kelsey's Human Development textbooks that I have never fully progressed through adolescence. This has gnawed at Julie for the past 29 years as she is apparently bothered by the fact that she basically married the Tom Hanks character in Big. Of course, Kelsey totally gets it. She often says to Julie, "Mom, you just have to treat Dad like he is a 12-year-old. Then he is fine." How wise my adult daughter is.

With Brett home until just after Christmas and Kelsey still in college, it might appear that my empty nest fantasy is only delayed until January. That however is not the case because of the huge parenting mistake that we made in 2007. I want to close this year's letter with a word of caution that will hopefully stand as a warning to those parents who have not yet made this mistake. Here is my warning – "Don't ever make this huge mistake!"

You may remember that after her successful brain surgeries last year Kelsey took full advantage of her situation and convinced Julie and I to get her a puppy. There it is, the huge mistake – getting your adult child a puppy. It is only a matter of time before you have to admit the mistake and acknowledge that the new dog is yours. So, in 2008 we acknowledge this huge mistake: Cubby (pictured in Kelsey's arms for posterity) is now our new dog! Note that Julie and I did not want a new dog - we wanted the empty nest. Not only didn't we get the empty nest, we got the worst dog in the world. He is a mix of a Pug and a Beagle – and has the worst traits of both. He whines, howls and chews up everything – he is stubbornly not yet fully house trained at 19 months. I have had many dogs in my lifetime, but Cubby rises above them all as a pure sociopath. He just doesn't care about anything, but his own spur of the moment desires and he has absolutely no interest in pleasing anyone.

JULIE HERE: AM I THE ONLY ONE WHO THINKS THAT IN MANY WAYS CUBBY IS A LOT LIKE TED?

166

Cubby is the kind of dog that deserves to be put in a sweater in the Christmas picture. As punishment for making this huge mistake I am certain he will live to be 23 years old.

Worst of all Cubby terrorizes the Grand Dam, our nearly 11-year-old bulldog Ginger. This year's Christmas picture captures Ginger at her happiest since Cubby arrived. Her face reflects the joy our entire family feels with Cubby now in our lives. "Don't ever make this huge mistake!" You have been warned. Merry Christmas and Happy New Year 2009!

OUR LOVE TO YOU ALL!

Ted, Julie, Brett, Matthew, and Kelsey

Made in the USA
Lexington, KY
06 May 2019